If It's LOVE You Want,

Why Settle for ^just SEX?

*How to Avoid
Dead-End Relationships and
Find Love That Lasts*

Laurie Langford

PRIMA PUBLISHING

© 1996 by Laurie Langford

PRIMA PUBLISHING and colophon are trademarks of Prima Communications, Inc.

Library of Congress Cataloging-in-Publication Data

Langford, Laurie.
    If it's love you want, why settle for just sex? : how to avoid dead-end relationships and find love that lasts / by Laurie Langford.
        p.   cm.
    Includes index.
    ISBN 0-7615-0309-9
    1. Sexual ethics for women.   2. Single women—Sexual behavior.   3. Premarital sex.   4. Man-woman relationships.   I. Title.
HQ32.L36   1995
306.7'082—dc20   95-49245
                                                                                      CIP

96 97 98 99 DD 10 9 8 7 6 5 4 3 2 1
Printed in the United States of America

Pseudonyms are used throughout to protect the privacy of the individuals involved.

How to Order:
Single copies may be ordered from Prima Publishing, P.O. Box 1260, Rocklin, CA 95677; telephone (916) 632-4400. Quantity discounts are also available. On your letterhead, include information concerning the intended use of the books and the number of books you wish to purchase.

*To my dad, who inspired me
through his own recovery.*

Abstinence makes the heart
grow fonder.

Contents

A Word from the Author

Many readers have strong religious beliefs that give them their primary reason for abstaining from premarital sex. I acknowledge and honor those beliefs, but I also want to address the millions of women out there who are not deeply religious.

Throughout this book, I use the term "sex too soon" frequently. This term is used in a generic sense. Each woman must decide for herself what the term means for her, based on her religious and moral beliefs. By discussing the sexual choices we have, I am not advocating premarital sex. This book is intended to offer information to all women, of all beliefs and backgrounds, without judgment.

Acknowledgments

I've been very fortunate to have many friends, family, and mentors who have helped me with this book. I thank the following people:

My agent, Jeff Herman, for believing in me from the start and for finding a publisher for the project.

Deborah Adams, for the special attention and time that she gave the project. Her insight and intuition were invaluable.

All the staff at Prima, especially Georgia Hughes and Andi Reese Brady, for their professionalism, enthusiasm, and expertise.

Friends and family members who helped edit the manuscript: Shelley Griffiths, Sandi Cox, Donna Kesl, Jill Siegal, Debbie O'Brien, and Garth and Sandi Smith. Thanks for your willingness to help.

My dear friend Michael Gelfand, for all that he has contributed to this book and to me personally. Michael was the first person to actually encourage me to write this book. His assistance in shaping and editing the manuscript was key, and his continuing generosity and friendship is very much appreciated.

All the men and women who shared their stories with me. Their honesty and openness were requisite in making this book helpful to others. And to the women in my Saturday afternoon women's group.

Helen Andelin, for providing the initial inspiration to write my own book. Her books literally changed my life.

My family: father, brothers, stepmother, aunts, uncles, and cousins. You have been supportive and encouraging, and I love you all very much.

Introduction

Deciding when to allow sex to be a part of our relationship is one of the most important decisions we will ever make. Many of us know from experience that sex has a profound impact on a relationship and on our emotions. If sex occurs too soon, the entire dynamic of the relationship can be altered, not to mention our emotional well-being.

Practically every woman I know wants to find one person with whom to share her life and raise a family. We long to feel secure, cherished, and loved. But we often find ourselves with a series of relationships that start out very passionate and yet end up painfully mediocre. They either fizzle out after eight or nine months, or they drag on for years without any real purpose or direction. The happily married life we once envisioned for ourselves seems more and more elusive as the years roll by. What is even more painful for many of us is that most, if not all, of these relationships are sexual. So often we feel taken for granted—we share so much of ourselves, yet it all seems for naught. Then, in addition to the emotional strain of going from one relationship to the next, many of us have religious and moral conflicts with having sex before marriage or, in some cases, without love. We may have justified our actions for various reasons—loneliness, wanting to connect with another human being, thinking the relationship was further along than it really was, and so on. *But now we are at a place in life where we want more.* We need to break the cycle (or as Susan Powter says, "Stop the insanity!"). We need to stop being sexual with men we don't love or have no future with. No more shame, guilt, and heartache. We will always experience some pain in the relationship, but we can eliminate the gut-wrenching, devastating pain that can result from having sex too soon. We may not know exactly what needs to change, but we have an inkling that a large part of it has something to do with the way we conduct ourselves sexually.

Very few of us learned how to handle this delicate part of life from our parents. Perhaps we were brought up with the idea that waiting until marriage was proper. But we usually found ourselves left with little instruction as to how one actually does that (and would we have even listened?). There are many factors to consider: our hormones, men's hormones, foreplay and how far one can go, social norms and peer pressure—the list goes on.

If It's Love You Want, Why Settle For (Just) Sex can serve as the mother-daughter talk you may never have had, or didn't listen to, or have long forgotten. All of the things I wish my mother would have discussed with me in order to prepare me for a relationship are in the following pages.

There are countless books, tapes, and videos out there on how to have a better relationship; how to communicate better; where to meet men; how to look, act, date, and mate. But the bottom line is, if you don't know how you are going to handle the sexual part of a relationship, the rest is pretty useless. It's as if you have a car and a destination planned, but no car keys. This book contains the keys you will need to approach relationships with confidence.

We are going to study relationships from a new perspective—one that closely examines the *sexual* aspect. We will see that *by first becoming clear about how we are going to conduct ourselves sexually, we will solve many of our relationship problems.*

There are essentially two parts to this message. The bulk of the book explores how to have a relationship without getting sexually involved too soon and provides a detailed look at how casual sex affects us and our relationships. The second part presents the principles involved in awakening true love and creating the relationship of our dreams.

Although this is a how-to book with practical advice, the process through which we may absorb the information can be very emotional. It requires a lot of soul searching and introspection, and most of all, a lot of honesty. Looking at these issues can be difficult, even painful. But I'd like you to remember that you don't have to actually *do* anything at this point if you aren't ready. You are simply gathering information and studying your options. Then, if and when you are ready, you can begin to implement these ideas.

If It's Love You Want, Why Settle For (Just) Sex can benefit single women of all ages and backgrounds who are not getting the love they want and who would like to learn more about the sexual options available. This is not to imply that one has to have had several casual relationships in order to qualify. If you have had only one sexual relationship in your life and it involved sex too soon, then you can gain much understanding from this book. Even if you never have had sex, you can learn valuable techniques that will help you create the love you want. Or maybe you are in a sexual relationship right now, and you have no remorse, pain, or frustration. Nothing inside of you longs for more. You are completely satisfied with your decision to be sexual in a relationship. This book can still help you improve your relationship.

No one wants to admit that their relationship is based on sex rather than love. No one wants to admit that they had sex too soon. We'd rather blame our relationship problems on our not being right for each other (which may be true) or his being a jerk (which also may be true). *But could it be that choosing to be sexual too early in the relationship is the culprit of our failed or stagnating relationships?* As we explore the sexual aspect of relationships and the mistakes we often make, we will see what part we have been playing in the demise of our own happiness. We will see how by having sex too soon, we create a very tenuous situation for ourselves.

If we make ourselves too vulnerable too soon, we fail to build a solid foundation for our relationship. Our relationship lacks structure and substance. We often don't take the time necessary to fully know the person with whom we get involved. We rush into a relationship with blinders on and then regret our decisions later. We don't nurture our relationship and make sure that it is based on love, trust, and respect.

How we conduct ourselves sexually makes a certain statement about who we are. When we have casual sex we are essentially saying, "I am willing to give all of myself to you, even though I barely know you. Your charm, your words were enough to convince me."

How we deal with our sexuality certainly has changed over the years. Many women feel that the message of the Sexual Revolution convinced them that "free love" was the way to go. When the Pill came out on the market, millions of women immediately jumped on the bandwagon. It was said that modern women were at last as free as men to enjoy sex without the fear of getting pregnant. The idea was to eliminate the double standard, making it acceptable for both genders to enjoy sex equally and to have it more often. The new attitude was, "If it feels good, do it." Then the focus shifted. Being a great lover became the issue, more so than whether or not we should have sex in the first place. Essentially, sex became expected and ultimately seen as casual. What was ignored by the many who bought into this notion was that sex does not affect men and women in the same way. I believe casual sex is unfulfilling for both genders, but for women in particular because they tend to bond emotionally much more so than men.

It's time we reevaluate our options and allow our internal voices to determine what our true standards are and should be, for our own well-being.

The only reason I felt qualified to write a book of this nature is because I have diligently been searching for the answers to these very questions. I have gained most of my knowledge from personal experience. Over the years, I went from one relationship to the next, wondering what I was doing wrong. The pattern of my relationships became tiresome. I was able to break out of the pattern finally by making a decision to abstain from sex until I marry. It was one of the best decisions I ever made.

Several years ago I taught seminars in Los Angeles for women on relationships, and I found that other women felt as I did. They, too, wanted to put sex on the back burner, at least until love had been developed. But the problem was, they didn't know exactly how to have a nonsexual relationship. They either felt that men wouldn't accept it, or they simply lacked the confidence needed to say no. As I researched the subject, I found plenty of books on how to have great sex but none (outside of Christian books) on how to *not* have sex, at least until you are ready or married. I saw a tremendous need for this message, and so I wrote this book.

I am not a psychologist. I'm simply a woman who, like you, has been through a lot and who has made choices that didn't work. But I learned from these mistakes, and now I have a desire to share what I've learned with others. I hope the information in this book helps you become clearer about your options and helps you approach relationships with more confidence.

The answers I share came to me through various avenues: books, people, and experiences. And all of these avenues, I believe, came to me through prayer. I was able to ask how to turn my life around and to be given the knowledge I lacked in my relationships. These answers are all within you as well. I'm not going to tell you anything that you don't already know. I'm simply going to remind you of what you know deep down inside.

If you apply the principles outlined in this book, you will be able to foster the kind of love you usually see only in old movies. Regardless of what your dating life was like before, after approaching relationships as suggested here, you will have more men of the caliber you're looking for and who share the same values as you do, pursuing you more than ever before. Men will find you more fascinating and intriguing. Men of great strength will see you as the same—a woman of great strength. They will want to know what makes you tick and what makes you different from all the rest.

In time you will find a good man, and, with hope, he will strive as hard as you do to make the relationship great. But what men do is irrelevant from the perspective of this message. Although you will want to find a man of high quality and character who is also compatible with you and your nature, he does not have to agree with your new-found knowledge, nor does he have to play much of a part in the process. *You* will be the one who decides if you're willing to accept who he is and what he has to offer in a relationship. Once you make your choice, you will then have the ability to awaken his feelings of love and honor, as well as his overwhelming desire to share his life with you. Love and marriage will no longer seem out of your reach. You alone hold the keys to your happiness.

1

Love Is the Goal

Before examining the problems that arise from having sex too soon, we need to look at what we are working toward. We must have a goal in mind, a reason for our diligence and our willingness to change. If there isn't anything to look forward to, then why put ourselves through the process? If we or our relationships are not going to be improved, then why go to the trouble?

One of the most important reasons to abstain from casual sex is for our own spiritual and emotional well-being. How can we possibly expect to have a healthy, fulfilling relationship with a man if we suffer from the low self-esteem and despair that comes from having sex too soon? The ultimate goal is to create the kind of love you have always dreamed about—one that is strong and lasting and that requires feeling good about yourself.

When a man deeply loves a woman, he responds to her differently than he responds to everyone else. He may be harsh with others, but with her he is tender and gentle. He has an overwhelming desire to make

1

her happy and to fulfill her heart's desires. When she walks into the room, he lights up. She brings him tremendous happiness, joy, and contentment. He feels as though he can't live without her, and he certainly wouldn't want to try.

Helen Andelin, author of the best-selling book *Fascinating Womanhood,* describes this as *celestial* love. She points out that even though a man might say "I love you" to the woman in his life, do nice things for her, or remember her birthday, this doesn't necessarily constitute celestial love. She writes, "Celestial love is more intense, more spontaneous, and dynamic than passive actions. . . . When a man loves with his heart, he experiences a deep feeling within. It has been described as a feeling almost like pain. He may feel enchanted and fascinated. In addition, he feels a tender desire to protect and shelter the woman he loves from all harm, danger, and difficulty. Then there is the deeper, more spiritual feeling almost like worship."

Isn't this what we long for and desire above all else? What good is it to achieve greatness in other areas yet lack this kind of love? These questions should be kept in mind as you continue reading. This is your vision, your light at the end of the tunnel.

Love Creates Security in a Relationship

Women need to feel secure in a relationship, and *love* is the foundation that creates that feeling of security. I know married women who do not feel secure because they do not have the complete love of their husbands. If we do not feel confident in his love for us and in the commitment we have made with him, our happiness is limited.

How to create this kind of love is largely what this book is about, but before we can even begin to discuss the principles involved in awakening true love, we need to see how sex affects relationships. If sex enters the relationship before a solid foundation of love has been established, then quite often we destroy our chances of ever building this kind of love and obtaining complete happiness. The only way our hearts truly can open up and fully experience the joy and freedom love offers is if we feel secure in our relationship. But to create the foundation of love, trust, and respect takes time and patience. It requires many hours of long conversation and undergoing many different experiences together. The process may take several months before you realize the two of you aren't a match or before tender feelings have been established.

If sex occurs before the foundation is built, we lose our balance and become insecure. We lose control of our emotions, and our judgment is altered. It's much more difficult for us to assess him, our true feelings, and the possibility of a future together. But if we choose to *postpone* sex until we receive confirmation for ourselves that we should continue in the relationship until love has been established, and until commitments have been made, then our relationship will be supported by a more solid foundation. We will be able to discern who he really is, what his true intentions are, and what we really feel about him. And we can do so without the uncertainty and fears that casual sex can create. We will still experience many emotions, and we can still be spontaneous in our relationships. But we won't experience the emptiness, the doubt, and the void that we sometimes feel when sex comes too soon.

Sex is a powerful and sacred experience. The act of making love is one of the greatest gifts we have in this life. Through this incredible act, we are actually able to create other lives! This is something we all know, but I believe we sometimes forget this awesome fact. When we make love to another human being, we come together as one and bond in the most intense, profound way. We share a very special, private part of ourselves. The last thing we want to do is take this sacred experience and cheapen it by making it too casual. One man I know said, "Many people see sex as no more than a handshake today." It's sad, but true. It's time we establish a different perspective when it comes to sex. Sex is obviously more than just a pleasurable experience that occurs between two people who feel like doing it, whenever they choose.

Let's analyze three different women and their experiences in order to see how they chose to approach the sexual aspect of their relationships. The following examples illustrate how having sex too soon can affect us and our relationships. We're going to look at their relationships, what they wanted, what they have, what the problem is, and what they could have done instead.

Carolyn

Carolyn was twenty-two when she met Ron.

"The first night Ron and I met we were in a club, and we talked all evening. I gave him my number, and I believe we saw each other the next night or soon after that. After our first date, he invited me over to his place. I said no because I knew it was the 'right' answer since it was only our first date. I really liked him, so I didn't want to ruin it. He was a perfect gentleman. He didn't push me at all.

"The next time we went out, we stayed out very late and I had a lot to drink. Again he invited me over. This time I accepted. It's funny, but I actually felt okay about saying yes then, because after all, I had said no last time. It's as though in my mind, I thought I had resisted for a long time, even though it was only one date!

"From that moment on, we were what Ron called, 'glued together.' We almost never left each other's side. That's partly why I didn't have a lot of remorse after becoming sexual with him so soon. I thought to myself, 'This is great! Finally, a man who loves me no matter what and doesn't just leave me after he gets what he wants.'   .

"I moved in with him almost immediately. It seemed like we had been together for years, and yet we had only known each other for a few weeks (that was a recurring feeling in my relationships). Living together seemed like the thing to do because, after all, we were together constantly, and Ron wasn't proposing marriage (there was no way *I* would make that suggestion). Also, we were in love—or so I thought.

"Ron could not and would not say I love you. I didn't want to say it until he did, but why wouldn't he ever say it? We were so intimate with one another, wasn't it only natural that we would verbally express our feelings? When I finally couldn't stand it any longer, I confronted Ron about his feelings. He told me he just couldn't say something if he didn't feel it. He cared for and loved me as a person but that's as far as he could go. What a blow! Even though he did care for me, I thought we were in love. I thought that's what two people who were making love and living together were all about. I was wrong. The only thing I ever wanted in life was to be loved. I thought I finally had that, and now in one split second, it all became a fantasy. It wasn't real. I cried and cried. (Of course he didn't see that. I wasn't going to let him know how I felt.) I tried so hard to figure out what went wrong. But did I move out? Not until a year later. I was too afraid. Where would I go? I'd be all alone, with no one to be there for me. Even though he didn't love me, I felt I desperately loved him.

"Then it became my mission to win his love. It didn't matter that he wasn't right for me (something I discovered later). It only mattered that I turn the situation around. In time, he did tell me he loved me. He grew to love me. He was very good to me in many ways. He was very generous financially. He showered me with gifts. He was fully committed to me in the sense that he would never consider going out with anyone else. We made a promise to each other that we were exclusive. We enjoyed many things together. Ron was very complimentary and was always building me up to our friends. He was a *nice guy*. But I still felt like I was a guest in his house. It definitely wasn't *our* house. When the subject of marriage came up (I finally *did* bring it up), he said he just wasn't ready, or he wasn't interested in getting married, or that his finances weren't in order enough to get married.

"I thought things would change. But they didn't, and I found myself becoming more and more bitter and angry. I thought, 'I'll show him! When I save enough money to leave, he'll be sorry!'

"Well, the day came when I did leave, and he didn't stop me. He did express sadness, but he didn't come after me with a marriage proposal. It took me a long time to get over that relationship."

What Carolyn Really Wanted.   Carolyn wanted to get married and have a family. She expressed to me her desire to be loved and cherished. She *didn't* want to get stuck in a relationship that wasn't going anywhere for over a year. Nor did she want the lack of love she experienced.

What Carolyn Had.   Carolyn had a relationship with a good man who grew to love and care for her. Yet, he didn't cherish her; his love was not deep and solid. Even though they agreed not to see other people, clearly something was missing. Ron wasn't willing to make any promises because his feelings hadn't been developed enough. They seemed to be just "playing house." Carolyn had a false sense of security. It appeared that she had it all—a nice home to live in and a kind man to share her life with. But she didn't have the things that mattered the most to her: true love and security.

The Problem.   Carolyn approached this relationship in the best way she knew how at the time. She honestly felt okay with the way things were progressing because they *were* progressing. After all, they went from dating to living together—that seemed like a major jump to her. Her self-esteem was such that as long as he showed continued interest, she was happy. She said no to sex on the first date because she knew it was the correct thing to do, not because of her values. She hadn't established her values yet. When she met Ron, she could tell he was a good person, and they hit it off so well that she thought it felt right. But she didn't take the time to find out or discuss what Ron really wanted in a relationship, what his goals were, or what his true character was.

Moving in with him without any further clarification of these points didn't help the situation. She still felt lonely and empty in the relationship. Carolyn didn't have the basic understanding of how to nurture the relationship and awaken deep feelings of love in her man. Therefore, Ron's feelings and level of commitment to her didn't develop properly. Perhaps they weren't meant to be together but that would have become obvious with time—before making the commitment of living together.

I should add here that there were many potential reasons why a woman might end up in a similar situation. She may have been very young and naive at the time. Maybe she came from a dysfunctional background that seriously damaged her feelings of self-worth. Maybe she was just going through a bad time. Even more likely is that she honestly didn't know things would turn out this way. She had high hopes (as we all do when we enter a relationship) that it would bring her lasting happiness.

It's important to understand why we make these choices so that we can learn from our mistakes and understand ourselves better. But even more important is what we are going to do about it now. Are we going to learn from our mistakes or continue the pattern?

What Carolyn Could Have Done.   First and foremost, prior to any long-term commitment, a woman needs to develop her self-esteem. Then she will care about herself enough to be very cautious as to whom she gets involved with. She wouldn't settle for mediocrity and lack of true commitment.

It would be easy to blame the relationship problems on Ron. You could say that he was afraid of commitment or that he wanted the convenience of a sexual relationship without the responsibility that comes with marriage. But Carolyn chose to become sexually involved (and therefore emotionally bonded) with Ron before establishing a commitment for the future and before Ron was in love. She has only herself to blame for the shaky foundation that ultimately fell apart. She should have acknowledged that relationships take time and have established her own sexual standards. Then, she would choose to wait to have sex until the two of them became committed, engaged, or married.

She would devote her efforts to getting to know Ron. Not just superficially, but over a long period of time. She and Ron would have explicitly discussed the kind of relationship they wanted with each other and the level of commitment they were willing to make. Later, as she ascertained that she wanted to be with him, she would confidently and peacefully trust in the process of building love and in her sound knowledge of how relationships work. Carolyn *would* get the love she has always wanted.

*T*onya

Tonya met James one year ago at a party. Within two months they had sex. Tonya said that they found themselves unable to hold back in the heat of the moment. The atmosphere that night had been very romantic, and they had plenty of chemistry. Even though they have been in a committed relationship for a year, the relationship isn't what Tonya had hoped for.

"James spends almost every night with me, although he keeps his own place. I've suggested that he give up his place and just move in, but he refuses. I love having him with me every night, but I hate the fact that we almost never go out. He says he's extremely busy with his career, which limits his free time. I usually end up spending the weekends alone or with girlfriends.

"I really love James, but he can make me crazy! He sometimes doesn't call when he says he will, he's often late, and he's not very affectionate when we are out in public together or around his friends. But what can I do?"

Despite having been together for a year, the topic of marriage has never come up. Tonya doesn't feel comfortable raising it because she doesn't want James to feel pressured. She knows that the mention of marriage might scare him away, and intuitively she realizes they aren't at that point yet. Tonya is very patient. She just takes it all in stride, hoping that in time, things will change.

What Tonya Wants.   Tonya wants to get married and have a family. She wants security and to know that her partner will be there for her forever.

What Tonya Has.   Again, it's interesting to see how what we want is sometimes very different than what we have. Tonya thinks she has a relationship, but what she really has is a sexual partner who *at times* treats her with tenderness—which is what keeps her locked in. Most of the time, however, Tonya is neglected and mistreated; she finds herself lonely and frustrated. She doesn't have the sincere love of her man, even though he may be loyal to her.

The Problem.   As usual, the problem began in the beginning of the relationship. Tonya and James became intimate in the heat of the moment, not because they consciously made a decision to be together in a monogamous relationship. They ended up being monogamous, but more out of convenience than anything else. Neither of them had anyone else in their lives. They liked each other, and they had had sex. So being together was the obvious result. But it was less than adequate in Tonya's mind. She had sex with James without any kind of discussion about where the relationship was going and what his intentions were. Essentially, she agreed to enter into a "situation," where she had very few rights, without any solid hope for the future. Several months had passed before James felt the discussion of commitment was even appropriate even though they were having sex. Tonya felt as though she gave a lot more than she received, and she was right. She gave far too much, too soon. Then, by continuing to give of herself yet receive the treatment James gave her, her feelings of self-worth was seriously affected.

What Tonya Could Have Done.   Tonya found herself in a sexual relationship with James because she didn't know what her standards were from the beginning. It could be said that perhaps she didn't have any standards, but I believe she wasn't in touch with them. Sometimes we choose to forget who we are, or we're in the process of finding out. Once we do determine what our values are, then we can strive to be true to them. Tonya hadn't become clear on these issues yet, therefore she was more vulnerable to sexual advances.

It could also be said that Tonya knew what her standards were—but hey, she's only human. Romance and emotions aren't so logical and calculating! But the issue here is, *Tonya wants the kind of love I've described. She wants marriage.* And as we'll continue to see, having sex blindly in this way will not give her what she wants.

Theresa

Theresa is involved with a married man. It isn't that she wanted to get involved with him, it just happened.

"I was so tired of being alone. I've been single for many years and it isn't often that I meet someone I like. I just wanted to get close to a man. I wanted that male-female interaction. Along came Jack. We sort of bumped into each other, and we developed a great friendship. You never plan these things, and, of course, I resisted any kind of involvement because of his marriage. But how could I resist for long? He was so warm, nurturing, funny, sensitive, and extremely sexy. We began having a sexual relationship after a couple months. Now he comes over when he can. I know he's not going to leave his wife for me, but right now I don't care. I just love the intimacy we share when we are together. He says things that really show he cares. He tells me how much he enjoys seeing me and how he misses me when we're not together."

What Theresa Wants.   When I asked Theresa what she ultimately wants, she said marriage. She told me how hard it is to accept Jack leaving on vacations with his family. *She* wants to be the one who plans a vacation with her own husband. She wants to share her life with someone on a daily basis, not just whenever he can get away for a moment, primarily for sex.

What Theresa Has. It's pretty clear that Theresa has a relationship based on sex. They have other interests, and they do have a certain amount of companionship, but even Theresa admitted that it's the sex that keeps him coming back. They don't go out, which really hurts Theresa. But she doesn't want to lose what she considers intimacy.

The Problem. Theresa is in denial of her situation. She thinks she's getting enough of her needs met to be comfortable, but she admits profound frustration. Theresa is clearly settling for much less than what is possible for her. Yet, she doesn't see it that way. She has told me many times that although she may not be getting the relationship she had always wanted, she does have a lot more than what she has had for many years. She wants to be loved, and this is the closest thing she can find for now—but settling for this relationship may be preventing her from meeting a man who is available to really love her.

Whereas Theresa used to want love and marriage for herself, she has now become obsessed with simply having satisfying times together with Jack. Her focus is now on when he will call or *if* he will call. It isn't even about finding a man for herself anymore. Jack gives her just enough to keep her hooked.

Theresa convinces herself that it's better than nothing. But when she describes what it's like in between the times she sees Jack, it's no picnic. She's elated when she sees him, but when he leaves, a pattern begins to emerge. She waits for him to call. He never seems to call when she wants him to or expects him to. Then she's full of despair. She feels depressed and hurt. She begins to pull herself out of it and becomes strong. She convinces herself that it doesn't matter and that she doesn't need him. She tells herself that she's not in love with him. Just when she becomes okay with the whole situation and regains her strength, he calls. She's drawn back into the entire cycle all over again.

What Theresa Could Have Done.   The solution lies more in building Theresa's self-esteem in order to feel worthy of true love. She honestly doesn't believe she's worthy of a real relationship. She doesn't believe it can or will happen for her. Rather than finding ways to get what she wants, she settles for so much less. She knew what she was getting into with Jack, but she didn't know how to prevent herself from getting involved with him because emotionally she wasn't strong enough. Essentially, she rationalized and justified a very destructive situation.

As she directs her attention to building her self-esteem and making room for a healthy relationship, she can break the pattern.

◇◇◇

Although each of these stories are very different, there are some clear similarities. All three women desperately want to be in a relationship. Yet, their desire to connect with someone overpowers everything else.

Two out of the three women expressed that they knew they were with the wrong person. It wasn't so much that they were only together for sex. But sex artificially prolonged these otherwise doomed relationships.

Tonya may have been able to develop a beautiful, solid relationship with James had she set a different standard in the beginning but because a solid base wasn't established *first*, the relationship never seemed to be completely right.

All three women suffered from low self-esteem, which is apparent simply because they didn't ensure that their own needs were met. The saddest part of all is that all of these women yearned for love, yet none of them had it.

The One-Night Stand, Few-Weeks Stand, and Few-Months Stand

Barbara was feeling down and decided to go shopping. She meandered through the shops with a sullen look on her face. She felt hopeless about her future and wished something or someone would come along

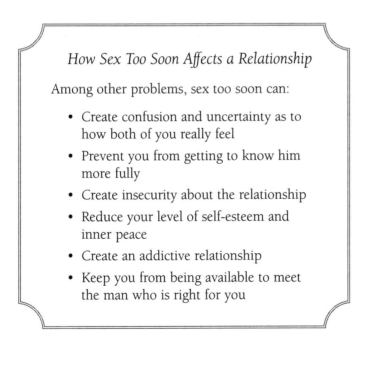

How Sex Too Soon Affects a Relationship

Among other problems, sex too soon can:

- Create confusion and uncertainty as to how both of you really feel
- Prevent you from getting to know him more fully
- Create insecurity about the relationship
- Reduce your level of self-esteem and inner peace
- Create an addictive relationship
- Keep you from being available to meet the man who is right for you

and make it better. That day she met Jerry, a handsome stockbroker.

He, too, happened to be shopping and as he glanced over at Barbara, he could see how somber and glum she was. He felt compelled to comfort her and walked over. He made a joking remark about the styles that were out and struck up a conversation.

In time they found themselves wandering through stores, talking. Barbara found it reassuring and pleasant talking to Jerry. She liked him, and even though they had just met, she felt comfortable accepting his invitation to have lunch.

They had a wonderful time and felt as though they had known each other for years. Barbara discovered that Jerry was visiting from out of town. When he offered to take her out to dinner, she readily accepted. (*Anything* to get her out of the funk she was in.)

Later that night, she met Jerry at the hotel restaurant where they had dinner. Jerry seemed so sympathetic and caring. She really felt that she could trust him. He opened up and talked about his divorce and the pain he had gone through. As the night wore on, Jerry invited Barbara to his room to have a nightcap. She felt completely comfortable with the idea at this point.

The next morning when she woke up, she looked over at Jerry and for a moment, panic set in. "What have I *done*?!" was the first thought that came to mind. After they dressed, he said he would love for her to come to Boston to see him, maybe even as soon as next week if she could. Barbara said she'd like that, and then she left.

One week passed before Jerry called. During that time Barbara was more depressed than she was before she met Jerry! She figured she'd been used, never to hear from him again. Jerry eventually did call to say that he was just too busy to have her come out yet. He said he'd call her when he came to town again. She hung up the phone, devastated. Not so much because she wanted Jerry but because she shared so much of herself, too soon.

✧✧✧

This example of a one-night stand can be applied beyond a single evening. Barbara and Jerry could have continued their involvement for several months, yet it still might not have evolved much beyond what they had from the beginning. Even couples who have been together for years can suffer stagnation of their relationship because they had sex too soon. These are the kinds of relationships that we need to avoid if we ever hope to build true love that lasts.

Also, Barbara was looking for someone or something outside of herself to take away her pain. She attempted to use Jerry as a way of getting out of her depression. Being in this depressed state, she was extremely vulnerable. On some level, she thought that getting involved with Jerry would make it all better, which obviously wasn't the case.

The Emotional Pain Sex Can Cause

Nothing is more painful than allowing yourself to be sexually vulnerable with a man, only to have his feelings and behavior change. Even worse is not hearing from him for days, weeks, months, or ever again. It's humiliating, degrading, embarrassing, and very hurtful. Yet we sometimes make the same mistake over and over again. We crave love and closeness. We allow our hormones to get the best of us. We become seduced by

> Women are not less sexual than men. But sex affects us differently. Women are more vulnerable than men. We need to protect our hearts and our bodies. Someone has to ensure that love and commitment are present before having sex. If there are men who share this standard for themselves, great. But our greater vulnerability means we need to make our own decisions independently.

a smooth talker who convinces us that we have more of a relationship than we really do. Maybe we vow to never do it again, but we still do not have a plan for how to handle the next situation. We still don't know how long we should wait, and we don't know what to do in the meantime.

Let me reassure you that you never have to feel this pain again. You never have to experience the heartache and remorse that casual sex creates. If this has been a pattern for you, then it's time for you to be excited about your future because by the time you finish reading this book, you will be equipped with the techniques necessary to break this pattern. Don't give up hope. You have the power to change and to create the life you've always wanted.

Being Honest With Ourselves

Part of the process of change is being honest with ourselves. Admitting that our relationships weren't what

> By saying no to sex without commitment and love, we are creating the opportunity for men to seriously consider what their true feelings for us are. They actually have to sit back and think about their intentions because they know casual sex isn't a possibility.

we thought they were can be painful. We think that if we admit they were based on sex rather than love, then we are really losers—unlovable and wretched. But being honest is the only way out. It's like being lost in a jungle with no idea which way to go. Someone comes along and says, "This is the way back to civilization. Follow me." But the road he says we must take looks so dark and ominous. We want to know if there might be another path, one that seems less threatening and rocky. But the guide shakes his head, and lovingly, yet firmly, says, "This is the only way for you to find true freedom. It may be rocky in places. You may be frightened at various turns. You may want to turn around many times. But in the end, you will be thankful you took this path because it really is the only road leading to where you ultimately want to go." I might add that the path I'm presenting in this book is far less difficult and painful than having a series of sexual relationships that never lead to marriage. It's the unknown that is truly frightening.

It isn't difficult to determine if our relationships may be based on sex. We can *feel* it. To help clarify your own feelings, ask yourself the following questions:

Do you often doubt his love for you?

Do you feel you give so much more?

Do you often feel taken for granted?

Do you feel that he maintains you as a sex object rather than a potential lifetime mate?

Does he resist committing to you even though you are having sex?

Is he unwilling to marry you even though you have been together a substantial period of time?

Does he resist saying, "I love you" even though you have been in a sexual relationship for awhile?

Does he say "I love you" strictly as a means of holding onto you?

Do you find yourself feeling angry and resentful toward him or men in general?

Are you sick of living like a gypsy, staying at his place then yours?

Do you sometimes feel lonely even though you are in a relationship?

Do you sometimes feel that it's the sex that keeps you together?

   If you find yourself nodding yes to one or more of these questions, you may be settling for a lot less than what's really possible for you. In each case, the cart is before the horse. The attachment is to sex, not love. By acknowledging the truth in your own relationship, you are well on your way to change. You have to know that what you have is not necessarily what you want. And you have to believe that you do deserve more. None of us has to settle for less than the highest form of love.

Do You Find Yourself in "Situations" Rather Than in Relationships?

Sometimes our relationships are more like "situations." By situations I mean just about anything other than a normal, committed relationship with someone you see as a true, potential mate. It's easy to tell if it's a situation. All you have to do is ask yourself the following questions:

Are you embarrassed about your involvement with this person?

Do you keep it a secret from your friends and family, possibly only telling a best friend?

Do you know there is absolutely no future with this person yet remain out of convenience or what you may be getting out of it (which could be strictly sex, financial security, companionship, protection)?

Do you know deep down inside that there is something not right about the situation?

Do you know intuitively that this person is somehow "beneath" you?

Is he involved with another woman (either married, seeing someone else, or just getting out of a relationship)?

> Relationships are complex, and sex isn't always the culprit of a bad one. But as we understand some of the possible consequences of having sex too soon, we can at least avoid certain pitfalls and begin by setting a healthier, more positive tone for the relationship.

If you answered yes to any of these questions, you may have a pattern of getting stuck in situations rather than building real relationships. A therapist can sometimes help us determine why we create these patterns in our lives. We want to determine why we made the decisions we made so that we can quickly find *solutions* and become available for a real and meaningful relationship.

I know people who feel it takes years and years to work through these issues, and perhaps it does for some. But it doesn't have to. What it takes is a *decision*. Of course, you can't make a decision to change a pattern if you aren't even aware of the pattern. But once you've gained the self-awareness, all it takes is a commitment to change. It isn't easy, but it is possible. We do not have to be victims of our pasts forever.

The following vignettes are from interviews I conducted with women to illustrate their feelings about sex and what it means to them. You may not relate to all of them, but we can all learn from other's experiences.

> I didn't lose my virginity until I was nineteen years old. I was known as a "good girl." Then I went off to college and slept with several men, one after another. I was out of my normal surroundings, so I guess I was more vulnerable. I confused sex with love. I wanted

love, yet I didn't. I was scared to death of it. I slept with so many sleazy guys, all of whom didn't want a relationship either. I didn't feel good about myself to begin with, so sleeping with a bunch of losers proved what a nothing I was. I could say, "See, I am a loser! Even the *losers* don't want me!"

✧✧✧

Sex has always been a way for me to get what I want. I thought because of my good looks and sexy body, I could pretty much manipulate any man into giving me what I want. I ask myself all the time, *"What was I doing?"* I ruined my life in a way and for what? Some attention? A good time? Gifts, money, trips? All I really ever wanted was love. But my pride wouldn't allow me to admit that. Deep down, I longed for a family of my own, just like my sister has. I often watch her with envy. She seems to have everything I've ever wanted. Her husband adores her. They take care of each other. Sex is just a part of their relationship. I guess I never truly believed I could have something that good. I had sex for all the wrong reasons. It had nothing to do with love, it was only a tool.

✧✧✧

I've never actually thought about what sex means to me—not in any detail, that is. I've just accepted the fact that it's part of a relationship. It's just something that happens when the time seems right. Now I'm reevaluating if this is smart. I have to admit, I don't want to continue having sex with several more partners. I'd like to settle down with just one man.

✧✧✧

I know this sounds crazy, but I find myself getting sexually involved with men I would never consider

marrying. That seems safer. If I were to meet someone with real potential, then I'd try very hard to do
everything right. But I haven't had much luck with
that. It seems like it's always the *next* woman these
men seem to change for and end up marrying.

Is a Good Relationship Possible
If You Have Sex Too Soon?

A relationship is not necessarily doomed just because
you have sex too soon. You may suffer from feelings of
remorse or your self-esteem may be affected, but the
relationship may end up being the best thing that ever
happened to you. Stewart and Gina are a perfect example of this. They fell in love almost immediately.
Stewart knew very quickly that Gina was the woman
for him, and even after they had sex, he felt the same
way. They were together constantly from that day forward. There was no discussion of commitment or
love. They even ended up getting married.

Camille and Kevin dated for a couple of weeks and
had sex without having a prior discussion. Today they
have a great relationship. They really seem to love
each other.

So how did these two couples succeed where so
many others fail? In these cases, both couples were
very much in love with each other *before* they ever became physical. They both knew it was more than just
a passing fancy. They just failed to verbalize their feelings before they had sex. Sometimes two people meet
and it's almost like destiny. They know they were
meant to be together. They both feel secure in the
other's feelings.

The question is, how often does this happen? How
often have you felt he was your destiny only to dis-

cover that he's now part of your *history?* It's a huge risk to take, especially considering that this is one of the most important decisions of your life. If you feel that

---

Separating Fiction from Fact

False Assumptions	THE TRUTH
• If you become intimate, he will feel committed to you.	• Sex has nothing to do with getting a commitment or gaining a husband.
• Sex has to be a part of every relationship—it's just the way it is.	• Without at least a verbal commitment to be exclusive, you have nothing concrete.
• You have to be sexy to get a man.	
• Once you have sex, it's automatically a relationship.	• Great sex may keep him there for a time, but it's not as important to him as you think. It won't necessarily keep him interested in you.
• If the sex is great, he will never leave you.	
• You will get a man to love you because he will become so dependent upon the sex.	• Sex does not have to be a part of every relationship. You do have a choice.
• Most men aren't willing to have a relationship without sex.	• Sex (especially if it occurs too soon) is not what will make a relationship great, lasting, or loving.
• Sex is just a physical experience—there are no emotional elements.	• Sex does not affect men in the same way that it does women.

strongly about each other, then it won't hurt to at least discuss the future and his intentions.

The Sweet Rewards

Waiting to have sex until you marry or develop a solid foundation of love, trust, and respect has many rewards. As you read through the list that follows, imagine what it would be like to experience these feelings consistently. Whenever I feel particularly frustrated with the lack of physical contact in my life, I turn to this list. It gives me great comfort and helps me to remember why I've adopted this philosophy. It's so easy to get caught up in day-to-day living, wondering what the point of it all is. But as I reread the following words, I regain my strength, and I am once again grateful for my decision. I hope this list inspires you as well.

You Will Create a Place for True Love to Grow

- The two of you will not be preoccupied with sex.
- The relationship will not be sabotaged by having sex too soon.
- It will be easier to determine true feelings and eliminate much of the confusion sex can create.
- Your relationship will be based on love, respect, romance, and trust.

You Will Be Protected

- You will be able to determine what his true intentions are and you will weed out the men who aren't serious.

- You won't be overly vulnerable too early in the relationship. You will feel secure.
- You are protected from sexually transmitted diseases and unwanted pregnancies.

Your Self-Esteem Will Grow

- You will gain self-respect.
- You will gain peace of mind.
- You won't feel like a sex object or that your relationship is based on sex.
- You will be in control of your relationship.
- You will experience freedom from within.
- You will feel good about yourself and experience more confidence than ever before.
- You will be free from guilt and fear.
- You will feel good about being true to religious convictions.

You Will Become More Attractive to Men

- You will stand out as unique and special.
- You will be seen as a disciplined, thoughtful woman.
- You will gain tremendous respect.
- You will be seen as someone who cares about herself physically, emotionally, and spiritually.
- You will be more radiant as a result of gaining peace of mind and happiness.

Note: There are obvious dangers with having sex at all, such as sexually transmitted diseases, not the least

of which is AIDS. If you are going to have premarital
sex, protect yourself by having "safer" sex. Only abstinence is completely safe, but using condoms can reduce the physical risks.

> Waiting to have sex doesn't necessarily
> guarantee that true love will grow. Some-
> times, no matter what you do, a particular
> relationship is not going to work, even if you
> do obtain a commitment, or even get mar-
> ried. Waiting does, however, create an oppor-
> tunity for true love to grow.

2

The Ten Most Common Mistakes Women Make

After talking to many women and looking at my own relationship history, I have discovered some very clear patterns in our experiences and in the choices we make. Following are the most common reasons we become sexually involved too soon.

Mistake # 1: We Go Out With Men Who Are Not Right for Us

This is probably the most common mistake of all. As they say, love is blind. But sometimes a feeling is not love at all. It could be lust, a weak moment, loneliness, or timing. Maybe you liked his eyes or the way he danced. Maybe he said all the right things. Whatever the reasons, we do not take the time required to learn the important things about a man before becoming sexual with him. We end up getting physical, and then a year later we find ourselves going through another breakup.

Sometimes getting serious with Mr. Wrong can cost us a lot more than time. No one knows this better than Susan.

The most devastating relationship for me was with a man I met several years ago. We had sex fairly soon, and I ended up getting pregnant. In those days, you got married. He asked me to marry him, I quit my job, and we made plans for the wedding. Then he announced to me one day that he couldn't marry me because the girl back in his hometown was also pregnant. I couldn't believe it! Here I was planning on marrying this man, constantly thinking about it, feeling good about the fact that our baby would have two parents, and then he changes his mind about marrying me. And he is with another woman to boot! I was so traumatized, I didn't know what to do. I was deeply wounded. I sometimes wonder if I'll ever be able to trust again.

I had an abortion. I still haven't been able to forgive myself for that decision. I know I've got to let go, but it's not easy. I feel it also contributed to even more self-esteem problems. I felt unworthy of love. After the abortion, I got on the Pill and began sleeping with a lot of different men. I just didn't care anymore. I felt I was a slut because of what I had done and because he had left me. I couldn't possibly be worth much, right? A whole vicious cycle was created that has been extremely difficult to end.

I found myself attracting men who were abusive because of how horrible I felt about myself. That's the only reason I was able to sleep with men I barely knew and who didn't love me. Since I didn't care about myself, why should they?

I gave sex to get love. Even though I essentially enjoy the physical act of sex, I primarily did it to feel loved. When I look back on my past relationships, I realize that it usually wasn't love I was receiving, but at the time, I wanted to believe it so badly that I suppose I convinced myself it was love.

I hate to admit it, but I have settled for very little in my relationships. Sex has connected me so strongly to men that I have convinced myself that I was in love with them when I really wasn't. We had no connection outside of the bedroom. Through sex, we were able to avoid being honest with each other and avoid talking about what really mattered. But you can't stay in bed all the time.

You May Have a Pattern of Getting Involved with the Wrong Men If:

- You find yourself losing respect for him. You do not appreciate his values, the way he conducts himself, or his thoughts and opinions.
- You fight over silly, little things that normally would not bother you.
- You often find yourself irritated with him.
- You find you have very little in common outside of the bedroom.

Note: You could still be with the right man even though you are experiencing some of these problems. But incompatibility is a strong possibility. Honest communication is in order if there is a relationship to be developed or salvaged.

We Ignore the Red Flags

In almost every relationship men will give out clues or signals or even direct statements about how the relationship will be. One man I dated, who was off traveling all the time said, "But I told you this is the way it would be from the beginning!" We get so caught up in the romance and the passion, we ignore the signs and sometimes even the words.

When I first met this same ex-boyfriend, I felt better about myself than I had in a long time. I felt that I was ready for a serious relationship and that my heart was open. He was handsome, successful, fun, and adventuresome. He was also kind-hearted and loving. I loved the fact that he really listened to me and cared about how I felt. I wanted to do everything right this time, and I did not want to ruin this relationship by having sex too soon.

He was a true gentleman; he didn't pressure me at all. We hit it off so well, and we were also very attracted to each other. We waited for what seemed an eternity to make love, but in reality it was only a few weeks. I told him I needed to know that we would be exclusive and that our relationship was heading toward marriage. He had basically been a confirmed bachelor up to that point, but his feelings were strong enough for me that he agreed.

Our relationship was fantastic in many ways, but I began to feel very lonely. He was traveling a lot, and he seemed to need a lot of what he called "alone time." He assured me often how much he loved me, but it did very little in the way of comforting me. What I wanted was *him* and his complete love and devotion. He did not want to discuss marriage. He felt pressured and told me that it was just too soon to discuss that kind of commitment, although we had been dating for several months. Meanwhile, it was okay with him to continue having sex on a regular basis. I could never figure that out. Why was it acceptable to be sexual, yet not be sure you wanted to spend your life with that person? He couldn't see the correlation. Now I understand that many men feel this way because they simply do not fully understand how sex can affect a woman.

Sometimes I spent the night at his house and sometimes I slept at my place. The nights we were together were great, but the nights I had to go back to my empty apartment were very lonely. I remember crying myself to sleep many nights, experiencing pain and confusion. Why did I always seem to find myself in these relationships? Why didn't he want me to be there with him every night, forever? It just didn't seem right.

The months dragged on until eventually we broke up. He admitted he never wanted to get married and he really didn't want children. It was the hardest breakup I have ever experienced.

I recently had dinner with this ex-boyfriend. Our relationship ended several years ago, but we have maintained a friendship. He said, "Laurie, we had a beautiful relationship, and you know it. I was very good to you. We shared a lot and we had a lot of fun."

I had to think about that for a moment. Was it really that much fun? And even if it was, was I seeking mere "fun"? The truth is, I didn't have that much fun. True, at times it was wonderful. He gave a lot, but he couldn't give me what I truly wanted—a commitment. I wanted someone with whom I could grow old and raise a family. I wanted to know that we would be together every night, not just a few nights a week. This certainly wasn't his fault, he was just being himself. He didn't share my same values, and he gave what he was capable of giving. I'm the one who chose to remain in a relationship that I should have known was wrong for me.

Now as I look back, it's a good thing that this man and I didn't marry each other. We really weren't compatible. First, he didn't want children. Another red flag was the intense loneliness I began to experience. The biggest lesson I learned from that relationship was that I need to take more time to determine compatibility rather than jumping in blindly. We should always take notice of the red flags that warn us to look before we leap.

Ask Yourself These Questions in the Early Stages of Dating:

Does this person want the same things I want in life?

Is this person ready for a serious relationship?

Is he capable of opening up and loving me?

Is he a nice person?

Do I like this person?

Does he have integrity?

Mistake # 2: We Don't Know What Our Standards Are

I want you to do something that may be very uncomfortable. Think back on your past sexual relationships. Go over exactly what kind of discussion occurred before becoming sexual. I do not necessarily mean right before sex—it could have been several days before. Try to remember what you talked about or agreed upon (if anything) before sex. Did you verbally agree to be exclusive? Did you discuss how you felt about each other (aside from expressing physical attraction)? Did you discuss a possible future together and your role in a future together? Or did you just assume that you knew the answers to these questions?

Most of us have been on autopilot for a long time. We may not have even considered that there are other options. But there *are* other options, regardless of any previous lack of self-examination.

We All Have Conditions

Conditions are a part of almost everything we do. Before being hired for a job, you are required to prove your worthiness. When you go to a restaurant, you are required to pay the bill and behave in a civilized manner in order to avoid being thrown out. Before accepting you into their buildings, landlords can require a credit check, a security deposit, and references. When you go to a bank for a loan, they don't just hand over the money because you are cute or you look trustworthy!

Why would it be any different in relationships? In our case, our assets are our hearts, feelings, and futures. When we are willing to have sex without any kind of commitment or expression of love, we are essentially saying, "I am willing to share the most intimate part of myself with you without really knowing who you are or what your intentions are."

Anna never gave her own standards much thought:

It is amazing, but I never considered that there should be a discussion of any kind before having sex with a man. I just always figured I would do it when I'm ready. I thought that if you had sex early in the relationship, you could get it out of the way and then enjoy the relationship. We could relax, the pressure was off, and I didn't have to worry about it. But after awhile, I always felt like I gave a lot more than I got in return. Now I'm beginning to wonder if maybe this has been the reason my relationships haven't worked out very well.

Anna might not be the only victim. Our lack of standards can actually harm our partner because we do not give him an opportunity to give to us. His motivation is lost because of our neediness. He pulls away because he feels smothered, trapped, or just overwhelmed. As he pulls away, we usually get scared and try even harder by giving more, which is just the opposite of what we should do. The only solution at that point is to give less and allow him to also be a giver and pursuer in the relationship. Men cannot love and cherish a woman who is willing to give so much of herself—especially her body—without expecting love. *In order for him to fall in love, he needs to give of himself.*

You Need to Establish Standards for Yourself If You Say Things Like:

- I believe in having sex when it feels right.
- I think two months is a good length of time to wait.
- When he is calling me on a daily basis, I will feel safe having sex with him.
- When I can tell that he is only interested in me and is not dating anyone else, I will have sex with him.
- I will have sex with him when I just can't stand it any longer.

These statements are not *standards*, they are *intentions*. But intentions are not enough to protect you from having sex too soon. And none of these precepts are sufficient to ensure a solid foundation for a relationship.

Begin Establishing Standards By Asking Yourself These Questions:

Am I willing to have sex without a commitment?

Do I need to be in love before being sexual?

How long will I give myself to get to know someone well enough to have sex with them?

Would I prefer to wait until I am married?

If you don't consider these questions and come up with a plan as to how you are going to conduct yourself sexually, you become too vulnerable and susceptible to getting sexually involved before you are ready. You cannot expect men to live up to your standards if you do not even know what your standards are. (We will discuss the various standards that are available in chapter 7.)

I want to encourage you not to gloss over these questions. Take some time and seriously consider how you feel. Search your heart and soul to discover what's really important to you.

Mistake # 3: We Don't Know What We Want

If we don't know what we want, we may find ourselves ending up with something we wish we didn't have. In Anthony Robbin's book *Unlimited Power,* he writes, "When the mind has a defined target, it can focus and direct and refocus and redirect until it reaches its intended goal. If it doesn't have a defined target, its energy is squandered. . . . Knowing what you want determines what you will get. Before something happens in the *external* world, it must first happen in the *internal* world. There's something rather amazing about what happens when you get a clear internal representation of what you want. It programs your mind and body to achieve that goal."

Some people grow up never really thinking through what they want. They don't realize the number of options available to them. Some, on the other hand, know exactly what they want from the time they are very young. And everything seems to fall into place. But for most of us, it is a difficult, long process to decide what we want.

We are the sculptors, free to mold our lives into whatever we are inspired to create. Of course, we can receive inspiration from all kinds of sources: God, friends, family, books, school, or movies.

If it is a lasting relationship that we want, then we need to maintain that as our focus and take the necessary steps to make it happen. We may not be able to control when or how we will meet our mate, but we can do so much in the meantime. We can read books on relationships, attend seminars, and talk to couples about their relationships. In other words, we can better ourselves and make room in our lives for that person. God, the universe, or whatever your belief system is will take care of the rest. But whatever our approach and overall beliefs, we need focus. When we remain focused on reaching our goal, we create the opportunity and even the ability to achieve it.

Ask yourself: What is your dream? What are you passionate about? If you just aren't sure what your talents are, look back on your childhood. What were you doing as a little girl? What came naturally to you? I loved playing with dolls. I played with them for hours and always pretended to have lots of children. I loved to cook and even clean (I was a strange child). I also remember climbing on top of our old barn and singing *Delta Dawn* to my imaginary audience, which happened to be buffalo. I was a natural teacher. I would often gather up all the neighborhood kids (including my reluctant little brothers) and have some kind of workshop. Of course, I could never get them all to cooperate, so I usually ended up extremely frustrated! Now that I look back on it, I realize that *who I really am and what my natural talents are were revealed to me at a very young age.*

Each of us has a very important purpose or mission that we are to fulfill in this life. It's up to each of us to discover what that purpose is. It doesn't matter if it is grandiose or in the public arena. It could be simple and private. The important thing is that we do it. We need to discover what comes naturally to us and feels most comfortable—aside from lying on the couch eating ice cream. *Everyone's* good at that!

In terms of relationships, I find that most of us don't really know what we are capable of achieving. We may have had so many negative experiences or have seen such little success in the relationships of others that we believe we may not ever have it much better. Some women have never experienced what it feels like to be adored and cherished by a man. But I promise you, this kind of love is possible for us all. We all know at least one couple that has this kind of love, and if that's the case, we know it's possible for us.

Sometimes it's easier to figure out what you want by first determining what you *don't* want. Here are a few examples:

- I don't want to be alone forever.
- I don't want to be unloved, whether in a relationship or not.
- I don't want to be seen as just a sex object.
- I don't want a relationship that is based on sex.
- I don't want to go through life without having a family of my own.
- I don't want to dislike myself and not have confidence.
- I don't want to feel like I have failed.
- I don't want to be bitter and angry.

Every December, I buy a new journal for the following year. I sit down on or around New Year's day and write out all my goals for that year. Then, after six months has gone by, I review those goals. Sometimes I set new half-yearly goals at that point. At the end of the year I can go back to the beginning and check off the goals that were reached. I have journals that date back for years, and I love going through them to observe where I was and what my goals were. Sometimes it's frustrating to see that I didn't reach some of my goals but even that helps me to see what I need to work on.

When we set goals for ourselves, we need to be open and flexible when new opportunities arise or new inspiration hits us. However, this shouldn't prevent us from setting up goals in the first place.

Take a fresh notebook or journal and find a quiet place where you can spend about an hour or so to contemplate what you want your life to be like. Look at the big picture first, then get more and more specific. Pick one aspect and write it at the top of one page, for example, "Spiritual Goals." Then describe on that page what kind of person you want to become spiritually. Don't worry about writing down specific goals yet—just write out a description of what you might be doing, how it looks, how it feels to you, where you are. Then take another page and write "Physical Goals" at the top and describe those on that page. Include your spiritual, physical, emotional, social, financial, and relationship goals, and add any other ones that come to mind.

Now on another page, write "The Kind of Marriage I Want." Describe what your day might look like, where you might live, the kinds of things you and your husband might do, how many children you might have, how you treat each other, and what the general feeling is like in the home. In chapter 13 we will create a "Man Plan," which outlines what kind of mate you want but right now just describe the marriage itself.

Your goals will undoubtedly change over time. It is important that you remain flexible, but it is very helpful to have a good idea of what you want or what you envision for yourself. By having this road map for your life, you will be well on your way to getting what you want.

Mistake # 4: We Send Out the Wrong Messages

You may be saying you want to wait, but your body language and appearance may be saying something else. When we send out the message that we are sexy, we usually end up getting the kind of attention that puts us in compromising positions. Don't be deceived into thinking that men want "sexy." Men may *appreciate* a sexy quality in a woman, but it is not a requirement for marriage. Men who are serious about finding a wife put sweetness, loyalty, honesty, and understanding a lot higher on their lists.

Charlotte was always looking for an intense attraction:

> I had a picture of what I wanted, but I never even came close to having that. I said I wanted a nice guy who loved me, but I was trying to use my body to get him. I thought if I just lost ten pounds and put on a mini skirt, I would get the guy. What a lie! What I got instead was a venereal disease, two abortions, and a lot of heartache.

It's not our bodies that men fall in love with. It's who we are on the inside and how we make them feel. By sending out the wrong messages, we receive the wrong result. Once you truly make a solid commitment to abstinence, it is important that you get your actions in alignment with your words. Not only will it be easier for you, but men will also appreciate it.

We cannot send out the right messages if we don't know who we are. Jamie tried every persona in the book to try to get men to love her and want her.

> I wanted *connection*. I usually felt *disconnected* so I used men to try to connect, to get me out of my pain,

and to help create some motivation for myself. If he wanted a strong woman, I was strong. If he wanted a weak, submissive type, I would become that. The games I used to try to hook men rarely worked. My timing was always off. If I tried to come across like a sexy siren, he would be attracted to a real mousy type of girl and vice versa. It was a never ending source of frustration.

If you are ready to attract a man with whom you can spend the rest of your life, then the best way to do that is to be aware of the messages you send out. You may need to drop the sexy siren image and begin thinking like a true companion. I am not saying that only women who dress conservatively get married. But most men want to be able to take the woman they love home to their family and feel comfortable. They want to marry a mate, a partner, a woman who obviously cares about what her appearance and actions say about her as a person.

Do You Send Out the Wrong Messages?

Do I wear low-cut blouses, tight shirts, extra-tight jeans, and very short dresses and skirts? If so, why do I dress this way? Is it because I enjoy the attention it brings me, or is it because I need the validation from men that I am attractive?

Is the attention I receive from men healthy? Is it the kind of attention I ultimately want and appreciate? How do the men I attract treat me in general?

Do I send out mixed messages? Do I say I want a healthy, long-lasting relationship yet come on to men like a seductress?

Do I say I want to get married yet look more like I want to party?

Sexual Talk

The dangers of engaging in sexual talk are significant. You may not see what the big deal is; after all, you are only *talking*. But something very powerful happens when two people begin discussing sexual preferences or fantasies. Your minds begin to focus on the words, and eventually your thoughts lead to action. I don't know too many men who are able to discuss these things without eventually making some pretty strong advances. If he is the one instigating the conversation, simply tell him you are not comfortable having that kind of conversation. He may think you are a little up-tight at first, but eventually, he will gain respect for you. He'll know that he has to treat you with respect in the future.

Note: Some discussion of our sexual preferences may be beneficial once you have established a committed, monogamous relationship, and especially if you have determined that you want to be married. Although I don't feel it's always necessary to do this, discussing these issues can help you determine sexual compatibility. But discussing them prematurely only invites sexual pressure and frustration.

Mistake # 5: We Don't Consider the Consequences

Another mistake many women make is that they allow men—or the idea of romance—to sweep them off their feet. They don't think rationally, and then they discover it's harder to think clearly in the heat of the moment.

At times we get caught up in fantasies rather than focusing on reality. Mary is a good example of this:

> I just loved the fact that Martin found me so sexually appealing. He was so verbally and physically demonstrative. It made me feel incredible. Over and over he would tell me how beautiful I was and how he craved me. It made me want to make love to him just so I could hear those wonderful praises. I knew how to drive him wild, and I loved the feeling it gave me. I felt in control. I felt appreciated, adored, validated. I think I became more addicted to that *feeling* than to Martin or the sex.

Mary was not focused on creating a solid relationship that lasts. She was caught up in fulfilling a craving or a need within herself. She didn't think about the short-lived effects, she was strictly in the moment.

In many areas of life, going with the flow is a great idea. But not when it comes to something as serious as when you will have sex with someone. Be flexible in terms of where you go out to dinner or which movies you see, but not when it comes to your values.

Before Getting Sexual, Consider These Questions:

How am I going to feel after we have sex? What about after a week has passed?

What if I were to get pregnant by this person?

Do I trust this man well enough to bond to him?

Do I really love this person, or am I just "in lust" or infatuated?

Am I just doing this to fill a void or to get me out of the pain I am in right now?

Am I doing this for the right reasons? What are they?

Mistake # 6: We Allow Our Hormones to Get the Best of Us

Valerie is a "junkie" for the sexual gratification she gets from men.

> It's so difficult to wait! I rarely meet someone I'm attracted to and so when I do, we have a few drinks, he's saying all the right things, then he's touching me, and I melt. The pace that men move at today, it seems like it would be impossible to wait for very long!

Valerie says she wants to get married and be in love but after talking with her further, I discovered that she really does not want that. Not now anyway. She's not willing to do what it takes to make it happen. She still wants to believe that love will magically come about. Also worth mentioning is that drugs and alcohol obviously play a big role in couples having sex too soon. We lose control over ourselves. By the way—whether it's affecting your sex life or not—if you feel you have a drinking problem, I highly recommend Alcoholics Anonymous. It works because it's based on spiritual principles.

Sometimes it's not sex in particular for which we are longing. It is closeness and affection. We just want to be held, to be touched, and to feel close to someone. However, we forget that the intimacy we may experience today may last only a very short time and could be preventing us from finding the man with whom we could share the rest of our lives.

Sheila remained in sexual relationships that were not right for her:

> In many of my relationships sex seemed to make everything all right. Whenever we fought, rather than working through it, we made up by having sex. During sex, we were connected. We felt close, tender, romantic, loving. I felt whole and loved when we had sex. That feeling would last for a little while, but eventually, the emptiness returned.

Each of my ex-boyfriends looked great to me in the beginning. They were all charming, handsome (I thought so anyway), and intelligent. But I was more in love with the *idea* of being in love than I was in love with them. At times the chemistry can be so strong and the level of romantic intrigue so high that we literally lose our logical minds. We don't think about the future or the consequences. We don't think through the fact that we will bond emotionally with these men. And if they end up not being right for us, we will have a very difficult time pulling away.

Trisha had never been promiscuous in her life, but she found out how difficult it is to keep her own hormones in check.

> One night when I was out dancing, I met an extremely handsome man who basically swept me off my feet. I mean, he was *gorgeous!* I had never met a man I was so attracted to. I quickly became very infatuated with him. We danced all evening and eventually made our way back to my apartment. He had too far to drive and it was late, so I offered him my couch. Well, he kissed me and I thought I would melt. Then we sat on

the couch. He began asking me about what I like sexually. I guess I said the right buzz words for him because he picked me up and began carrying me back to my room. I kept saying no, I didn't think this was a good idea, but to be perfectly honest, I really did not mean what I was saying, not entirely anyway. My mind said no but my body said yes!

We had a wonderful evening and the next morning I drove him to his car. He asked if I was going to go dancing that night and I said yes. Later that night I saw him making his way toward me and when he reached my table, he put his hand out as if to shake my hand! My heart sank. After what happened last night, he now wants to shake my hand? I chose to ignore that gesture and gave him a hug. We danced, but after awhile he disappeared. He never called. I left several messages, but he would not return them.

I had never felt so stupid in my whole life. I knew I had been used and mainly because I allowed my sexual desires to overrule my logic. I always had been in control before, but I had never met a man like this before either. Next time I will know better.

Sometimes we may have the best of intentions only to find ourselves repeating our mistakes. It can be a very painful situation. *The desire to be true to our values has to outweigh our temporary desire for sexual gratification.* We need to keep in mind that one day we will be able to fulfill our sexual needs, but we don't want to fulfill them now at the expense of our happiness, health, and future.

Before Reacting to Your Sexual Desires, Ask Yourself These Questions:

Do I really see a future with this man, or am I just reacting to my hormones?

Do I find myself dwelling on sexual thoughts, which lead me to acting on them?

Do I want to forfeit building this relationship on love and commitment in order to have a few minutes of pleasure?

Am I putting myself in a situation where I can be swept off my feet—that is, lose control?

Mistake # 7: We Become Impatient for Love to Grow

Everything is fast these days. Fast food, faxes, E-mail, Fed-Ex. You name it, you can get it almost instantly. But love takes its own sweet time. Usually it takes so long that we just say, "Oh, forget it!" You know it's too soon to be sexual or intimate, but you just want to get on with being a couple. You cannot see waiting for months to build something solid. You somehow want to get into the express lane. This problem is what I call the Right Now Syndrome—we want it all *right now* so badly. The process of falling in love, getting to know the other person deeply, developing trust, and sharing a variety of experiences all take a tremendous amount of time. Considering who we marry and the success of our marriage are two of the most important aspects of our lives, being patient is a small price to pay.

But then we sometimes wonder if we are being selfish. We hate to see him feeling so sexually frustrated. We want to please him and give him what he wants. These are all very natural desires, and one day we will be able to fulfill them. We'll be able to experience the beautiful pleasure of opening up our heart and surrendering to a man worthy of our love. But if it is too soon, we are giving too much.

If we understand and apply the principles that awaken love, then we can be sure that love will grow. As with so many things in life, we can't rush natural processes. One night as I was lying in bed, I became very frustrated because I just couldn't fall asleep. I tossed and turned and tried to make myself fall asleep but to no avail. Then the thought came to me, *I will eventually fall asleep. There is no doubt about it in my mind. It is inevitable.* I felt the inevitability of falling asleep was a great metaphor for so many things in life. There are just certain things we can count on happening—in due time. But no matter how hard we may try to hurry the process, we are just spinning our wheels. Love is much the same way. We can only do our part and then the result has to be left to God and the natural process that is taking place.

Are You Using Sex Merely to Advance the Relationship?

Do I think that by having sex, the relationship will be stronger and more serious?

Do I think he will love me more if I have sex with him?

Do I want to have great sex or do I want a marriage partner? (By the way, you can have both, but not by putting the cart before the horse.)

Am I able to be alone, without a relationship and still be happy?

Mistake # 8: We Get Scared We May Lose Him

A healthy, happy relationship is almost impossible if we are operating from fear. When we become so insecure about losing him that we are unable to be true to our own feelings, then how can we possibly have a solid relationship?

If we lose a man because we won't have sex with him, then obviously he's not the right man for us. His priorities differ from ours. Being a companion and building a lasting relationship is not high on his list, not with you that is. That may be hard to accept, but we must move on. It is that simple. On the subject of abstaining, one woman I know made this comment: "There is no way men would ever put up with this! There are too many women who will give them what they want!" That's like saying, "Men don't really want to get married, so we might as well just live with them."

It is true that there are plenty of women who will have sex early on. But the choices other women make shouldn't have anything to do with our own choices. Besides, it doesn't take long for most men not only to get very bored with casual sex, but also to experience the emptiness of a shallow relationship.

Having sex with a man does not necessarily keep him interested. It may keep him coming back for awhile, but it doesn't necessarily keep him interested in you as a woman with whom he wants to build a life-long commitment. Men are not as interested in sex as we tend to believe, or as they might appear to be. Studies have shown that sex is usually closer to the bottom of the list of priorities for men than at the top. It's just that men are instinctively aggressive in pursuing women sexually. That does not mean it is the most important thing for them.

Ask Yourself These Questions:

Am I afraid that he won't be able to love me for me, without sex?

Am I afraid that if I don't have sex with him, he will leave me?

Do I sometimes feel as though all I have to offer is sex?

Do I sometimes feel like he only sees me as a sex object?

Do I place too much focus on the sexual part of a relationship rather than on getting to know him better?

Am I more concerned with how he is feeling about me rather than determining how I feel about him?

A fear of losing him has more to do with a low self-concept than a man's behavior. If a man is worthy of you and sees you as a potential mate, he will accept your standards.

Mistake # 9: We Lack Confidence in Ourselves and Our Decision

When our self-esteem is low, we may not feel worthy of being abstinent. We may think that all we have to offer is sex. We don't feel worthy of love, so we do everything in our power to sabotage the relationship. We don't realize that we do have a lot to offer and that we deserve the highest form of love there is. You may lack confidence in your decision to be abstinent if you:

- Continually change your mind about being abstinent

- Are easily talked into sex

- Are not clear about your reasons for abstaining, and you don't express them with conviction

- Don't feel comfortable being honest about your values

As we grow spiritually, and we become very clear as to *why* we want to abstain, our confidence grows. Remember: You are absolutely justified in wanting to protect your mind, body, and soul from the damaging effects of having sex too soon. You deserve more than what a strictly physical relationship has to offer. You are worthy of true love that lasts forever.

Ask Yourself These Questions:

Do I honestly believe that I have a right to say no to sex no matter how long I have been in the relationship?

Am I comfortable with losing a man who won't accept my standards?

Do I feel good about my desire to wait until I am committed, engaged, or married?

Do I feel comfortable expressing my sexual values to the man I date?

Mistake # 10: We Deceive Ourselves into Thinking That We Have More of a Relationship Than We Really Do

We want to be in a relationship and feel close to someone. But sometimes we hear what we want to hear and see what we want to see. Then we are heartbroken when a year later he says, "I never actually *said* I loved you! I said I wanted to get married, but I never said *we* would get married!"

Brenda fell hard for Blake immediately:

I wanted to get married so badly that I did not see him for who he was. I was so taken by him, all I wanted to do was marry him. We had sex within a few weeks. I have never been promiscuous, but Blake said all the right things. When I met him, he was so wonderful and charming. He was everything I ever wanted. I lost my mind and my emotions. It is as though I got drunk on his words, his touch, his energy. He told me he wanted to take care of me. He asked all the right questions, the kinds of questions that get you excited about the possibility of a future together, "Where do you want to live?" "How many children do you want?" "What kind of house do you want?" These questions gave me the impression that he wanted these things with me, and they made me feel more comfortable about having sex with him. But after a couple months, I found out he did not want those things with me, and he said he didn't feel like he misled me at all!

Ask Yourself These Questions:

Does he call you and ask you out?

Does he verbalize and express his love?

Has he made it clear that you are the woman he wants—not just sexually but in every way?

Is he consistent in his behavior toward you?

Are you going along with his direction because you are not really interested in a serious relationship?

If you answer no to any of these questions, don't be too alarmed. It does not mean the relationship is doomed or that things cannot change. The important thing is to be brutally honest with ourselves about the relationship and his feelings for us.

Whatever your circumstances have been, just becoming aware of your patterns can help you change the way you relate to men. You will begin to realize that you can create the relationship you want and that you don't have to be a victim of circumstance.

3

You Slept with Him:
Why He Won't Call

You have met someone new, and you're crazy about him. The minute the two of you met, you knew this was going to be something big. The first night you went out, you talked until two in the morning. He gave you a tender kiss on the cheek as he said goodnight. You couldn't sleep, you could think only of him. He called the next day to tell you what a great time he had and how he couldn't wait to see you again. You saw each other several times over the next week, each date more incredible than the last. You talked about the future and what both of you want in life. He said he had never met a woman as special as you.

Finally, you are both alone in his apartment and you are kissing. One thing leads to another, and you end up having sex. The next morning as you are getting ready to leave, he says, "I'll call you." You kiss each other good-bye, and the rest of the day you are on cloud nine. You can't stop thinking about him, reflecting on the night before. As evening approaches, he still hasn't called. You make sure you don't wander too far from the phone so you are sure to get his call. It gets later and later. You feel a little hurt. You go to bed thinking he must have been busy. Oh well, you assure yourself, he'll call tomorrow. But tomorrow comes and goes, still with no phone call. Now your stomach begins to knot. You feel more and more depressed. You wonder what he is doing and why he hasn't called. You are now unable to focus on your work or enjoy anything you do. You feel sick about the whole thing and wish you hadn't slept with him.

Maybe this man does call after three or four days have passed, or maybe he doesn't call at all. Either way, it can be devastating for a woman. We usually feel that by having sex, the relationship automatically moves to a new level and that if we feel more emotionally attached to him, he must feel the same way. So when he doesn't call, we get the message that we weren't that special after all. We feel deeply hurt and rightly so—we shared a very personal and intimate part of ourselves.

Almost every man and woman I interviewed told me that *women* become more emotionally attached than men after becoming sexual. There were a few exceptions, however, which I cover later in this chapter.

Sex Changes Everything

Sex radically changes a relationship because of the profound emotional effect it has on women. The problem is that many people—men and women alike—want to ignore this fact. They want to pretend that both sexes can simply enjoy sex without any ties as a purely physical pleasure. In truth, we just aren't set up that way as human beings. Sex affects men and women differently. Although there are exceptions, we need to stop pretending that we are emotionally invincible when it comes to sex. What's wrong with saying, "As a woman, when it comes to sex, I become bonded emotionally. Therefore, I have to protect myself and take greater precautions when it comes to whom I sleep with and when."

If we didn't bond so emotionally, we wouldn't feel used or taken for granted if things didn't work out. One woman had this to say, "Every man I have ever been with has made it very clear that if I wanted to use them for sex, to go right ahead. They seem to have no problem with the idea of having sex without any ties." Another woman said this: "Most men do not see a direct correlation between sex and love. They seem to be able to have relationships that are based strictly on sex. It's almost as though they know women who they might consider just for sex and women they would consider for a serious relationship."

I am not saying that all men are uncaring, sex-crazed animals. However, we have to be honest and face the difference between the sexes. One woman told me this: "I have never known a man who wasn't willing to have sex with me if I gave them the green light. As long as I'm game, so are they." Another woman said, "Men want sex, that's all there is to it. Maybe that isn't all they want, but if they have an opportunity to have sex with a woman, they are going to do it. They don't think in terms of emotional attachment." There are many men who may be offended by these remarks, but even men who don't think this way acknowledge that they know plenty of men who do. It's a fact of life.

Many men are unaware of these differences and that's partly because we haven't been acknowledging them ourselves. Even though they may have experienced this difference in men's and women's reactions several times, men usually don't understand why it's happening. They only know women usually freak out at a certain point in the relationship, become more possessive, and want more of a commitment. They may not consider that the reason women behave so differently after sex is because of a chemical reaction, which we'll explore next.

Why Women Bond More Than Men

Men sometimes don't call because they don't bond emotionally in the same way we do. You may be as relieved as I was to discover that there is a biological explanation as to why we become so emotionally attached through sex. *Oxytocin* is a chemical that is released within your body when you have sex. I first learned of oxytocin through Dr. Pat Allen, author of *Getting to "I Do."* As I continued researching the phenomenon, I found that this is the same chemical that is released when a mother nurses, which causes her to feel the overwhelming desire to cuddle her baby and bond with the child. Men have the same chemical released when having sex but not nearly to the same degree, which means most men do not become as bonded.

This explains why we may see him in a new light after sex, why we become more serious than he does, and why we usually long to cuddle more so afterwards than he does. It isn't because we are emotionally weak or undisciplined. It doesn't even have to do with the men we have chosen. It's part of our nature.

A friend of mine dated a man to whom she really had not been attracted. Somehow they ended up having sex, and once they did, he amazingly transformed before her eyes. He became her Adonis. She felt jealous if he went out with anyone else, waited for his calls, and broke plans with her friends to be with him. Yet, this was a guy she earlier had not even been interested in!

The problem is, we either forget that sex affects us so deeply, or we allow other emotions to override our judgment. The result is that we sometimes make choices that create a lot of pain for us down the road.

Donna

"I had just separated from my husband and my self-esteem was at a low point. I was so miserable I didn't want to get out of bed in the morning. I wondered if I ever would be in a relationship again. Then one day I met my new neighbor, Stan. He was really nice and easy to talk to. We became friends and began spending a lot of time together. We went to the movies and out to dinner. He called me almost every day. We developed a wonderful friendship in four months.

"I knew the relationship probably wouldn't go anywhere ultimately, and I was not in love. But I felt so needy at the time; I wanted intimacy. We became particularly close one night and Stan said, 'Are you sure you want to do this because I just don't know if we should.' All I could say was, 'Yes! We *should* do it! I *want* to!' And we did. I had no idea I was going to fall so head over heels in love with him. I just didn't plan on that happening. I thought I could remain in control. But I fell hard.

"I guess Stan could tell how strongly I felt and it scared him. We still spent time together, but I could feel him pulling back. He didn't want to take me to a Christmas party he had been invited to because he said he wanted to go alone and maybe even meet other women. He said he didn't want to be a 'couple.' He even said, 'Donna, we are not an *item!*' That really hurt, especially after all the physical closeness we had shared. He made it clear that he wanted space and that he didn't want the pressure or responsibility of a serious relationship.

"So we stopped having sex, and although we have remained friends, there seems to be no chance for a romantic involvement. It's very painful, but there is nothing I can do. I'm tired of trying to figure out what went wrong and why Stan didn't fall in love with me."

I hear stories like this every day and the most glaring point that stands out for me is this: We are settling for so much less than what is possible for us! In essence, we are settling for sex, even though it's love that we want.

Even though Donna told me that she bonded emotionally with every man she had been with before, it did not enter her mind that the same thing might happen this time. She assumed it was okay to have sex because of how well the two of them had hit it off, and she didn't think she ultimately wanted Stan anyway. Also, the fact that they waited such a long time (four months is a very long time these days!) made her feel even more secure. She didn't think it was necessary to talk about commitment. But Stan and Donna were a long way from being in love. They really liked each other. They were friends. But that was it.

When I asked Donna if she felt the relationship with Stan would have turned out differently if they had discussed issues such as where the relationship was going and their feelings about commitment, she replied, "If we had discussed all of those issues, then we would not have had sex."

And if they hadn't had sex, Donna probably would not have come on so strong—which caused Stan to pull away. They would have continued to build a friendship. Maybe they would have fallen in love—or maybe they would have simply remained friends.

Stan and Donna knew the answers to these questions before they had sex, they just didn't verbalize them. Neither of them were making any commitments and neither really wanted to. Which would have been fine for Donna—except that she became emotionally bonded as a result of having sex, and her feelings changed. She was the one who lost out in the end. Stan said that hurting her was the last thing he wanted to do, but he was not feeling more connected to her.

"I knew when I was having sex with him that I was taking a big risk, but I didn't care at the time. I was so lonesome. I had felt so rejected by my ex-husband that it just felt good to have someone else show that much interest in me. I was feeling ugly and old and I wondered if anyone would ever love me. And there was this nice guy who wanted to be with me."

Donna began to see that although she thought she was getting her needs met, she really was denying them. Her true needs never were met—what she got was a temporary fix and heartache.

Mindy

"I always thought (or hoped) that if a guy really cares about you, it won't matter if you sleep with him on the first date or the twentieth. My problem is I attract the wrong type of men.

"I met Steven at a party. He was sort of a "bad boy"—and very handsome. He wasn't my type, but he was so turned on by me, and that felt great. I liked the attention. So we ended up having sex the same night we met. After that, he did not call for a long time. I called him, but he was always busy. After the third time we slept together, he started taking me for granted. Then I found myself asking him for more time together, and he didn't seem to care about seeing me. That's when everything completely fell apart."

Mindy said it all in her first few words when she said she "hoped" that if a man cares, it won't matter when you sleep with him. She wanted to believe that she could sleep with a man right away and still have the relationship she had always dreamed of. She wanted to believe that if a man really loves her, he won't leave her. Unfortunately, it usually doesn't work that way. The love has to be created first, and that rarely happens on the first date.

Not only did Mindy realize that Steven was not her type, but a red flag went up right away telling her he was a "bad boy." So she opened herself up to being emotionally vulnerable to a man she couldn't trust.

Also, just like Donna, she did not anticipate bonding with this man. She knew he was not for her, but she went ahead anyway then regretted it later.

Jane

"Once I was very lonely on a New Year's Eve. I went to a local hang-out place and I ran into a guy I had seen before. We had sex right away. I asked him what his ideal woman was. He told me she had a face like Heather Locklear, a body like Dolly Parton, and a personality like Donna Reed. Well, here I was—my hair was bright red at the time, I was wearing black leather, I was an angry feminist (nothing like Donna Reed), and I was skinny (nothing like Dolly, that's for sure!). We were having a sexual relationship, and yet we didn't know each other. We obviously were not right for each other. I just figured, 'Oh well, it's too late. We are on this course now. We're a couple.' Since we were a couple, I began expecting certain things, like spending a certain amount of time together. I felt this bond, like I should be setting up house with him, but I didn't even like the guy! That's how sex affects me. I feel a bond, even when I don't want to. Our relationship wasn't tender, the sex was not like *making love*, it was just something we did.

"I couldn't picture myself taking him home to Mom and Dad, and I couldn't picture him being my husband. That's the most frustrating aspect—you get attached to him, and there is nowhere to put him! You can't plan a life together, so you are in a perpetual state of limbo. He eventually dumped me, which now that I look back, I'm grateful for because I just couldn't end these relationships. I felt too powerless.

"You can't ask for anything more because he has nothing to give, and you don't feel it is your right anyway. It's just a horrible place to be. I know a lot of women get very angry when men don't give of themselves financially, when they don't feel any sense of responsibility to them even though they are sexual together. But why should they? Men do not *owe* us anything. It's up to us to make sure our needs will be met *before* we get too involved with a man. We need to know that he is committed and there for us. The promise is equal—when we marry, we commit to being there for him also."

Have You Ever Felt Like These Women?

I am amazed at how powerful sex really is. It really does change everything. I can be friends with a guy, see him periodically, have no real ties, and be perfectly fine with that. But once I sleep with him, forget it. Then I want to be with him more often, and I begin to get real concerned about the relationship and where it is going. It's really awful, especially if there's no real commitment. Then I feel like I'm constantly trying to get him to care more. As long as you are giving yourself sexually, there is no going back emotionally.

✧✧✧

I didn't want to feel as though I was negotiating a business deal in a relationship, so I have always just gone with the flow. When I felt comfortable with the idea of sex, I would go for it. The problem was, I always felt like I got the short end of the stick. The men I have dated would never bring up commitment or marriage. It seemed like as long as they were getting sex, they were content. But I wasn't content at all. I want more in a relationship, and I'm not getting any younger.

✧✧✧

If I'm having sex with a man and he doesn't want to commit or eventually get engaged, I begin to feel as though he must not love me. If he loved me, he would want to make the relationship more permanent. That's hard to accept, but once you have sex, it seems like there is nothing you can do—unless you want to break up and start over with someone new.

✧✧✧

When I told my boyfriend I didn't want to have sex anymore, he said I was being silly and that I enjoyed the sex, too. But he's missing the point. In fact, many times I didn't enjoy it—not in the same way he did. I wanted him to love me and to want me forever. I wanted to mean more to him, but sex seemed to affect me on a much deeper level than it did him.

◇◇◇

I always convinced myself that I was using the men I dated. I saw how men could just have sex with women with no real emotional involvement, and I guess I figured if they can do it, so can I. But I honestly feel that I put up a huge wall to protect myself. I became detached.

Note: Remember that if you do not want to discuss commitment, feelings, and the future before having sex, that's your choice. But realize that you run the risk of bonding, thus changing your feelings and wishing you could go back in time to do it differently.

Three Exceptions to the Bonding Rule

There are a few times when women seem to be able to have sex with men and not bond emotionally.

1. *Women who seem to respond more like men.* These women usually have a strong masculine energy, even though they may also be quite feminine. They seem to be able to have sex without getting emotionally attached as men are able to do. Quite often, they are the sexual aggressors. They may have one or more lovers without any commitments and appear to be unfazed by it all. I see this more and more with women all the time. Many women today have the attitude that they've got all the time in the world to have fun,

enjoy sex, and avoid marriage. They are independent and carefree. But I believe it is rare when a woman truly feels this way. Even these women who seem so self-contained and invincible have been known to break down and tearfully express the pain they experience in relationships. They want to be loved and cherished just as much as every other woman.

Very few women are able to have casual sex for long without experiencing painful repercussions. Many women start out thinking they can handle it, only to find out they can't. Or, they think they can change the man's feelings. One woman put it this way: "When Jake told me he wasn't ready for a serious relationship, I figured I could change his mind. I wasn't all that concerned when we had sex because I thought it would turn him around. But it didn't."

In other words, even if we adopt a consciously casual attitude about sex, we are playing with fire. And besides, why would we want to have sex with someone who is obviously not right for us?

2. *When the sex is not satisfying.* There is a notion that if he can satisfy you, he can have you. If not, it is difficult to get you to surrender. Men instinctively know this, which is why they try so hard to not only have sex with you, but once they do, to please you sexually. It's not just for their egos, it's so they can win your heart and gain your devotion. They know if they cannot *move* you, you are going to be unimpressed. So, when the experience is less than adequate, it's fairly easy to walk away without any problem—in fact, we usually can't wait to get away.

3. *If you have had sex with him long before and you reunite.* You may have bonded the first time years ago, but the relationship did not work out. Over time, the emotional bond you once had diminished, at least partially. Then, you got back together and had sex. It just wasn't the same. Your feelings for him were not the same, and the entire experience just didn't work for you.

Sexually Aggressive Women

Let's look at some of the comments of the men I interviewed.

> Jared: I dated a woman who insisted on having sex fairly early in our relationship. She convinced me that it was okay, but I told her I wasn't sure I was ready. I suggested that we get to know each other better first because sex does change everything. But she really wanted to have sex. I guess I could have said no, but there we were in bed, naked, with the knowledge that if I didn't do it, I would be considered the biggest wimp of all time. The next day I felt very weird about the whole thing. I could tell she was feeling closer to me, but I was feeling more and more clear that the relationship was not going to work out.

It is interesting to see that Jared actually warned this woman of his feelings, yet she ignored his words and chose to go ahead anyway. Maybe she thought she could change his mind, or maybe she thought the sex would be so fantastic that he wouldn't want to leave. Either way, she is the one who ended up hurt. I asked Jared to further explain why he chose to have sex anyway, considering the doubts he had, and he said, "I didn't know I was going to feel that way the next day.

I was attracted to her, and I wanted a relationship so when she convinced me to go forward with sex, I thought maybe it would work."

> John: I have had a few relationships where we had sex without any commitment and after awhile we parted as friends without any bad feelings. But that has been a very small percentage compared to the number of relationships that ended badly because the women wanted more after having sex. I have learned that if I have sex with women I know are not right for me, they usually become much more serious after sex, and I feel less serious about them. I withdraw, and they're hurt. I don't know why this happens, it just does. It's a pattern I have become aware of recently, but for many years I was clueless. With one woman, I was concerned she was going to kill herself, she was in so much pain. But the interesting thing is, with almost all of these relationships, I was totally honest with the women. I told them I was very attracted to them, but that I did not love them. I made it clear that if they were just interested in a casual relationship, I was game. They all said yes, they wanted to get involved, and they too were fine with a casual relationship. But it never worked out that way. They became much more emotionally attached. So I learned that to get someone to sign on the dotted line is not enough because feelings can change. It's amazing, though, that these women seemed to want to have sex more than I did. In most cases, they were the aggressors.

Why Sex Too Soon Scares Men Away

These are some of the reasons men sometimes get scared away after having sex.

Women's Expectations.   As we bond with a man, we begin to have certain expectations—all of which are natural. We expect him, for example, to have certain feelings for us. We believe he loves us, or we think he should. We figure there should be a future together—after all, we just made love, didn't we? We expect him to treat us with more tenderness, more love, more concern. We expect him to call us consistently and include us more fully in his life.

These are pretty heavy-duty expectations for a man, even though they seem perfectly reasonable to us. It is very difficult for many men to sacrifice freedom and commit to one woman. The only thing that can get him to do so completely is a deep feeling of love for the woman. So you can imagine how utterly frightening it would be for a man to have these expectations placed upon him when he hasn't developed a strong love for the woman. Quite often he just wants to get away. And even if we don't verbalize these expectations, men can feel them. If we don't have sex, however, we don't project expectations, and we are able to give him the space he needs to fall for us.

The Challenge Is Gone.   We all appreciate a challenge. If we get involved with someone who so easily gives of themselves without some sort of challenge, we don't appreciate it as much. We may not like that fact, but it is the nature of all human beings. As Thomas Paine once said, "What we obtain too cheap, we esteem too lightly; 'tis dearness only that gives everything its value."

It isn't that we are *trying* to be a challenge for its own sake. What we are doing is taking care of ourselves and setting a higher standard. As a result of that, we naturally become more challenging to him.

Why would we want to do something that may clearly cause him to lose interest? Men would not think of buying us a diamond ring on the first date because it could seem inappropriate. They may *feel* like doing it, but common sense tells them to hold back.

In the very early stages of a relationship, both sides have to be very careful not to scare the other away by either wearing their heart on their sleeve or coming on too strong. Once love has been established and verbalized, everyone can be more free and just enjoy the relationship.

His Feelings for You Change. When a man feels that he can have you sexually without love or any other requirement, his feelings for you usually will change. Whereas in the beginning he may have felt intrigued and highly interested, if sex occurs before deeper feelings develop, he may begin to doubt his initial feelings.

What men tell me more than anything else is, if it was so easy for them to become sexual with a woman, then maybe it has been that way with other men. Men place a value on everything. If you are so easily attainable, they figure you are not worth as much as if they had to jump through some hoops to get you. This is another reason why we absolutely want to establish deep, loving feelings, including trust and respect—before we allow sex to enter the relationship.

Men Are Not the Problem

It is easy to blame men. "He lied to me!" "He led me on to believe there was more!" "He told me he loved me!" We feel like victims. We were sucked in by a real Casanova, and once he got what he wanted, everything changed. Therefore, it's his fault. How could it not be? *He* was the one who came on so strong in the beginning and made all those promises. What could *I* have possibly done, except for maybe being stupid enough to fall for it?

Of course, some men will make promises they will not keep and some will have incredible integrity. But as a rule, both parties need to make better decisions and be more considerate of the other person. The most important decision we can make is to take responsibility for ourselves and our actions. Do we want to be victims forever? Or do we want to take control of our destinies regardless of what others do?

Why Love Must Come First

Men sometimes feel as though they are backed into a wall against their will. They feel more responsible as a result of having sex, and yet they don't want that responsibility. If they were in love, it would be okay because they already would have wrestled with the idea in their heads and made a decision to be committed. Then they would willingly take on the responsibility. "What responsibility?" you ask. A relationship is a big responsibility for both parties, but men see it as a huge commitment of their time, attention, money, and emotions. They don't give those things up easily. Only a deep, solid feeling of love will persuade him to commit. In fact, once a man falls in love, he will *want* to make sacrifices.

4

Are There Men Who Will Wait?

A common misconception is that abstaining from sex, especially until married, is very unrealistic. The belief is that no one wants to avoid sex, most of all men. I believe nothing could be further from the truth! Oh, sure there are lots of men who will move on once they learn of your values, but there are plenty of men who will wait. In fact, many men are secretly wishing they could find a woman with high morals.

Just as there are all kinds of men out there, you will receive all kinds of responses when you say no to casual sex. Some men will be intrigued and find your standards refreshing. Others will see you as immature or even manipulative. It's best to expect the entire gamut of responses and be prepared to stand firm regardless of what men think.

When a man falls in love with a woman, he wants to make her happy. He is not obsessed with only having sex, although it may be a preoccupation. Of course, he wants to make love to her because that's one way for him to express his love. But if she conveys to him the importance of waiting for her emotional and spiritual well-being, in most cases he will accept her feelings. When a man is in love, it's the *woman* he wants. He wants her heart, and he wants to share his life with her. As I've said before, sex is not at the top of the list of priorities with most men—as much as it may seem otherwise.

A man wants a woman who cares about herself more than anything else. Not in a selfish, self-centered way but in a way that sends out the message that her body is not on loan to anyone, anytime, just for pleasure. He wants a woman he can cherish and love with his heart and soul.

I asked a close friend whether if he met the right woman, he would be willing to wait until marriage to have sex. This man has been married before, was very promiscuous when younger, is over thirty, and is not religious. He thought for only a moment and then said in a very serious tone, "Yes I would—if I really loved her and it meant that much to her." I was thrilled to hear him say that and not all that surprised. Lots of men have told me in confidence the same thing. (They may not admit it to anyone else, however!) Most men are not going to announce voluntarily that they would be willing to wait unless they, too, plan to wait. They usually don't know what they would be willing to do probably because they have never found a woman who challenged them in this way.

Here's what other men had to say:

I'm sure I would be willing to wait if I met a woman who felt that way. First, I would consider how strongly I felt about her, and if I loved her, I'd want her to be comfortable. If I knew there wasn't a possibility of a future together, I guess I'd move on. So I suppose it is smart for women to do this because most men will have sex with a woman if she's willing, even though they may have no intentions of going further in the relationship.

◇◇◇

I can't say that I would be willing to wait until I am *married*, but then again, I have never been so deeply in love that I felt I would do anything to have her. I guess I would have to be in the situation and then see how I feel. I definitely want to know that we are sexually compatible, but I have been in some horrible relationships where the sex was great, and I wasn't happy. So having a great sex life is not everything.

◇◇◇

If I feel a woman is telling me she doesn't want to have sex with me until we are married because she is just playing games with me, then I'm out of there. I don't like to be manipulated. But if she sincerely has religious beliefs or just plain morals that tell her it's the right thing to do, then I'm okay with that. I even respect that. But it has to be sincere.

◇◇◇

I have known women who said they wanted to wait but had sex anyway. Over time they made sexual moves on me, or they didn't stop mine. I guess they had honest intentions of waiting but changed their minds. It has caused a lot of confusion for me, and I end up thinking women just don't know what they want.

The Four Types of Men You Will Encounter

So much depends on a man's character, his values, his goals, and timing. He may respond one way now, yet react in an entirely different way a year from now. Some men are more sexually aggressive than others, some wait for you to make a move. It's really up to you to find out what kind of man he is, which takes a considerable amount of time.

Although many types of men are out there, I have chosen the four types that you likely will encounter as you date.

The Religious Man.   It really helps to date men who feel the same way you do about sex. If he has the same religious convictions as you, your life will be much easier. There are religious men who intend to wait to have sex until they are married, no matter what. However, there are also many religious men who may believe this is an ideal, yet do not always follow their religious path. But typically, if he meets a woman who says she wants to wait, the religious man will honor her wish and strive to maintain that standard.

If you say that you would rather not be alone in your apartment with him, for example, generally he will understand. If you find yourself going a bit too far, both of you will want to pull back and gain control. You will not be fighting the battle alone. This doesn't mean, however, that he will not try to make advances. After all, he is only human. But when you remind him of the implications, he usually agrees and tries to refrain.

The Respectful Man.   This type of man is very considerate. Although he may not agree with your beliefs, he cares about your feelings on the subject and vows to be respectful of them. Again, this doesn't mean that he will not make advances, but he typically won't hit the road simply because he's not having sex.

The Hopeful Man.   This type of man may give you a lot of lip service. He could still turn out to be quite kind, but deep down he really believes he can change your mind about having sex. Doing so seems to be his primary goal, even though he may also want a relationship. He pretty much ignores your words and continually puts pressure on you to get physical with him. With this man you feel more like a sumo wrestler than anything else. Eventually, he says he can't handle it and flies the coop. He may come back several times, however. He may even accept your standards at some point and turn out to be a pretty good guy. But each time he comes back, I guarantee he will put the squeeze on you. Be especially wary of the promises he makes to you. It will be ironic if each time he comes back, the romantic, loving talk about your future together will increase. Be careful!

The Insincere Man.   This man is out for only one thing. He wants you all right, but he sees you more as a big lollipop than a lifetime mate. Smooth and charming, he says all the right things and even spends lots of money on you. (It would be in your best interest not to allow him to spend a lot of money on you—you don't want to feel indebted.) He may even tell you he loves you very early on. You'll feel like you're in heaven. You may feel so secure with this guy, so convinced that his feelings are real, that you figure there would be no harm in being affectionate. But many hearts have been broken by the insincere man. When you tell him no, he sees it as an interesting challenge and will try every method in the book to get your clothes off. But he usually will not invest too much time because it just isn't worth it to him. There are too many women who will, so he decides to go after them. And that should be perfectly okay with you. The minute you pick up on the fact that you have met an insincere man, the first thing you should do is RUN! Life is hard enough as it is.

What Men Really Think About Sex

My interviews have revealed a variety of men at different levels of enlightenment on sex:

> Ted: I think most men are primarily interested in sex. If you look at survival of the species or procreation, the male in many species is very driven to have sex with the female. Most of the time the female doesn't allow sex to happen until she is ready; usually when she is ovulating. When you see an attractive woman, quite often you will see a swarm of men around her. It is within the male nature. So, I believe it is largely biological. However, I don't see that as an excuse not to grow as individuals. I'm trying to learn how to approach sex differently today. If I were to have sex with a woman today, I would consider whether or not I was willing to really be there for her, beyond just having sex. Sometimes I instantly know a woman is not right for me, although I may be sexually attracted to her. But I'm trying not to settle for just sex.

✧✧✧

> Calvin: I would discuss the relationship more, and where it is going, before getting physical. I want someone who is really there, who is strong, and who wouldn't do something they don't want to do just to please me. I want a real person who takes care of her needs and doesn't compromise her values. The only way a man is really going to respect a woman is if she doesn't allow him to take advantage of her. She needs to let him know that she is a real person with strong

values and important emotional needs that need to be fulfilled.

✧✧✧

Benjamin: Most men are very focused on sex, but sex is not really the most important thing to most of us. We want love, trust, and a partner. But the problem is, if sex is available to us, we will usually go for it. We feel it is our responsibility to please the woman and to give her what she wants.

✧✧✧

Eric: It may seem unfair, but I think women should decide for themselves when they want to have sex because I don't think men have as much risk as women do. Men can have sex without the fear of getting pregnant. Women also have a greater chance of becoming sterile as a result of sexually transmitted diseases. Also, men typically don't have to worry about a broken heart if a woman just uses them for sex. We don't have as much of an emotional investment.

✧✧✧

Carl: At one point in my life, all I was interested in was having fantastic sex with a woman. That's it, nothing else. I got involved with a woman I had met at work, and after our first date, we had sex. I knew I didn't want to see her again, and I told her so. She was livid, to say the least. She went home, vowing never to speak to me again. A few weeks passed, and we ended up getting together again. I guess we were both lonely. We didn't *acknowledge* that it was only for sex that we got together again, but basically that was the reason.

When I asked Carl why he told this woman he didn't want to see her anymore after the first time, he replied,

"I suppose I lost interest right away because she was conquered. Also, the sex opened up a new level of intimacy that I just was not ready for. The sex part is easy for me, but the intimacy part is a different story. Then you get into issues such as: Do I even *like* this person? Am I going to be open with her? Do I want this relationship to go somewhere? I didn't have the answers to these questions. I was so interested in having sex that I didn't really learn about her as a person."

Carl continued by telling me that what he wanted and what he got from relationships were two different things. "What I thought I would be getting as a result of having sex was a higher self-esteem or confidence. But instead, what I experienced was confusion, feeling I was in over my head, and that I had to make a commitment to this person who I didn't even know. So, what I thought would be empowering ended up being a self-destructive cycle."

Carl finally ended this cycle through a relationship with God and by entering into a healthy relationship with a woman. He is now engaged to her. "When I met my fiancee, she told me she was not interested in having sex for a very long time. She wanted to take things slowly and really get to know each other. I thought, 'How refreshing! What a novel idea!' I ended up falling in love."

Josh: I plan to wait until I marry. I was raised with these values so it's just been a part of my life. I feel sex is a gift from God, one that is shared with your lifetime mate. I know that most men don't feel this way, and they even criticize my values. But when I see men at work, at the gym, and basically all around me, who are getting women pregnant, contracting venereal diseases, and have all kinds of other chaos in their lives, I know I've made the right choice.

Many men *will* wait. But the bottom line is, we need to do what feels right for us, regardless of what men think about the issue. As we change, we will draw in a different kind of man—one who shares our same values.

5

So What If You're Not a Virgin? Re-Virginate!

For those of us who have had relationships that were based primarily on sex, it hurts to acknowledge that we have behaved in a way that contradicts our moral or religious beliefs. We sometimes see ourselves as "damaged." We think no one will love us or really want us. As we reflect on our past behavior, we cry with shame and remorse. We wish we could go back and do it all differently.

But we can't go back. We can't undo what has already been done. We have to embrace the pain. We have to feel the sadness and compassion for the little girl within us that was so desperately reaching out for love and validation. And then we need to *reestablish our standards*. If you have religious convictions, then repentance is in order. The point is to get your actions in harmony with your values.

What we *do* is not always who we *are*. We have to acknowledge that the life we used to live is not a reflection of who we really are. Our core—our heart and soul—is not interested and never has been interested in casual sex. Due to various circumstances, our actions were completely out of sync with our internal values.

We must accept what we cannot change. Once we reach this point of acceptance, we are able to reestablish our standards—those beliefs which we have lost touch with. Jasmine is struggling with this very issue. She comes from a culture in which a woman must be a virgin when she marries. When Jasmine turned twenty-eight, however, she found herself doubting her situation.

> I had just moved to the United States and I became fearful that I would never find a husband. Also, I realized I was completely inexperienced, which certainly wasn't the norm in this country. I guess I just gave up on the idea of waiting because of my fears. I lost my virginity to a man that I only saw for a short time. Almost immediately I felt so much remorse and guilt. I couldn't believe what I had done. I strongly regretted my decision. But it was too late. Then I fell into a deep depression. My self-esteem suffered. I found myself sleeping with several different men over the course of a year. I just figured there was no point in behaving any other way. I'm being more cautious these days. But I still can't help feeling that I will be seen as used goods to a man of my culture. Who will want me?

This is a very common experience for many women and it's a real shame! I know many people want to blame their religion or culture for creating guilt and shame. But it's the woman's *choice* as to what she ultimately believes. Many of these women do, in fact, share Jasmine's beliefs. Obviously, there are going to be negative repercussions when they go against those beliefs. But feelings of guilt can be *good*. They can be an excellent gauge to let us know when something isn't right.

We see from Jasmine's story how easily we lose hope for the future. Our self-esteem plummets, which leads us to even more destructive behavior until we honestly believe there is no way out. We see ourselves as unlovable and unworthy.

But none of these things is true. We may have been sidetracked, uneducated, blind, and maybe even foolish. But we are not unlovable or unworthy of the best that life has to offer. The solution is very simple. We simply reclaim our virginity. *Re-virginate,* as I say.

Being a virgin isn't just a physical matter. It has to do with our hearts and our desires. If we have a pure heart and an honest desire to establish a higher standard for ourselves, then we are essentially renewing ourselves from within. We are making a new beginning.

Reclaiming our virginity is just one aspect of this process. We also are reclaiming our souls and our bodies. We are choosing to care for ourselves on a whole new level, one that is more spiritually centered. We no longer have to suffer the shameful feelings; the guilt, the remorse. We can be free to love ourselves *and* another completely.

Re-Virginate and Be Proud!

Unfortunately, not everyone will be compassionate and understanding about our choice to re-virginate. Society has a ways to go before it will fully appreciate a woman who sets and maintains high standards for herself.

I have a friend in her mid-thirties who is a virgin. Many who know her feel it's a curse. She has had many frustrating discussions with people who can't understand her preference, so she has decided to keep it a complete secret. She has almost become paranoid about it. The last time she and I were discussing her virginity we were in her apartment and she actually leaned over and began whispering to me as though someone might hear her say the "V" word.

Just as we set a new standard in our relationship with a man, I believe we need to set a new standard with society in general. When and if those around us ask about our sexuality—presuming we even want to share our beliefs—I think we should be honest and proud. We need to express our belief in abstinence honestly without fear of ridicule. We are not asexual—in fact just the opposite is true! We see sex as more sacred and special than ever before. That's why we're saving it for someone very special.

Our stories may be private but our standards for waiting to have sex can be expressed with dignity and strength.

We All Have a Story

We each have our own reasons for wanting to make a change in the way we conduct ourselves sexually. Everything we've been through up to this point has molded who we are today. The choices we make in life are in part due to what we learned or experienced as children. Although we shouldn't justify unhealthy behavior as adults on our past, we can shed light on why we do the things we do. Maybe we became sexual with men we didn't love because we didn't get the love we needed as a child. We used sex as a way to receive that love. There may be countless explanations for why we are the way we are. But when we look honestly at our past, we are able to stop blaming ourselves and emotionally beating ourselves up as though we are terrible people. We are not bad girls trying to get good. We are simply trying to gain whatever knowledge we lacked, and we are attempting to make better, healthier choices.

I'd like to share my own personal story with you. I do this to point out that no matter what you have been through, you can start over. You can become the kind of woman you always wanted to be, and you can achieve the joy you so richly deserve.

My Story

On October 14, 1966, our entire family piled into our Ford pickup. I had just turned two years old. We drove along the old dirt road on the outskirts of town when we came to a train track. The red lights were flashing, indicating that a train was coming. My father stopped and waited for the train to pass. Once it passed, we proceeded to cross the tracks. We were then struck by another train, traveling the opposite direction on the second set of tracks. My mother (and the unborn child she was carrying), brother, and sister were killed instantly. My father was in critical condition, but survived. Amazingly, I had only a scratch on my toe. In one split second my life had changed dramatically.

I was tossed around between aunts, uncles, and my grandmother for a few months until my father took me to live with him. He remarried about a year after that. My father and stepmother had three sons together.

We moved approximately thirteen times, and no, my father wasn't in the military. He was an alcoholic.

As many of you know or can imagine, growing up in an alcoholic home was very unstable and painful. I hated everything about our existence. I spent most of my time alone in my room. Because of the problems at home and my own unhappiness, I began drinking a lot and running away from home.

There were times I would go home and attempt to live with my father. We spent a lot of time playing pool together in the bars. But his alcoholism was progressing rapidly, which made him more and more difficult to live with. Eventually, I ventured out on my own.

I was fourteen with no supervision whatsoever. While I should have been enjoying my youth, being carefree, I was weighed down with adult problems. *Surviving* was my main concern. In order to support myself, I played pool for money almost daily. Pool and the bars became a way of life for me for several years.

I wanted to belong and to be important to someone. I was starving for attention, and I found I could get it from men. But instead of love, I found exploitation. Years of pain and heartache followed. I felt I had nowhere to turn. So I did what many people do when they hit an emotional bottom. I cried out to God. I simply said a prayer asking for help. That help came, over time and through various avenues.

I quit drinking and decided to change my lifestyle. Everything was working in my favor. I took second place in a national pool tournament in Las Vegas. After that I quit playing pool, mostly because I wanted to stay out of the bars. It's difficult to abstain from drinking (and sex) when you spend most of your time in a pool hall. Those three things (drinking, pool, and sex) tend to go together. I share this part of my story only to point out that even an ex-pool hustler can re-virginate! If I can do it, anyone can.

At the time of the tournament I was twenty-one. I still had not re-virginated, however. I had a couple of serious relationships, but I invariably became unhappy and frustrated once we became sexual. Deep down inside I wanted to wait until I was married, but my low self-esteem told me that wasn't possible. I wanted affection and I wanted a relationship. I thought sex was part of the deal. I honestly didn't realize that I could say no, and even if I could, I didn't know how! No one prepared me for these situations and so I learned on my own—through trial and error. For the longest time I tried to justify my behavior and ignore my conscience. But I found myself miserable with the choices I was making until finally, I could no longer ignore my inner voice.

I decided to make a pledge to myself to abstain from sex until I marry. Then I asked God to help me maintain that standard. I got in touch with what my values were and I set goals for myself. I set out to learn about relationships and how they work. I practiced new behavior as I dated and I learned a lot. I began to see a tremendous difference in my relationships and in the way men reacted to me.

The peace of mind and personal joy that I have today as a result of these changes is immeasurable. I feel good about myself today and best of all, I don't experience the frustration and heartache that used to plague me. I feel as though I am finally equipped with the knowledge I need to make my own dreams come true.

I have accepted that I am a work in progress. What I've learned more than anything else is that I need to be kinder to myself. I need to accept who I am and where I have come from. I realize now that I am a beautiful person who has a rich background of life experience that makes me worthy of love—just like you! I am also able to use this experience to help others.

I have re-virginated and so can you. You can start over and create the life and relationship you have always wanted. It all begins with you believing that you are that beautiful person, worthy of love. Then, Mr. Right can do the same. Otherwise, he isn't Mr. Right. *Right?*

Write Down Your Story

Writing out my story has helped me tremendously. You might want to do the same. It doesn't matter if you're not a writer; no one else needs to see it. I'm not talking about writing a complete autobiography. Begin with your childhood. For instance, write how you felt about where you lived; how you felt about your parents, brothers and sisters, and friends at school. Write about anything that has significance for you. Describe yourself in detail, including your feelings, likes, dislikes, fears. Then make your way up to the present. Where are you today?

As you begin to learn more about yourself and your life, you'll awaken to a new level of consciousness. You'll begin to see yourself in a new light. I used to think I was a tough, street-smart girl, but when I began writing about what I was really feeling and thinking, I found out I wasn't as tough as I thought. I was really very much afraid. I felt alone and unsure of myself. I was a little girl trying desperately to be an adult. The growth that has come about as a result of examining my life has been amazing. I believe it's been an important part of the process that led me to re-virginating.

True Success Stories

The following women's stories can provide inspiration for us all.

*R*honda

Rhonda is a woman who had been sexually active for years but then decided to abstain until marriage. She was abstinent for eleven years until she met the man of her dreams and got married. "I believe that anyone can be abstinent until marriage if they have a firm belief that it is possible. Many people think it's unrealistic but if you get caught up in that way of thinking, you will only set up ways to fail. My faith in God is what really gave me the strength. If I just relied on my own power, I don't know if I could have done it. The desire for sex never goes away, it's just a matter of getting it under control rather than letting it control you. It will always be there, but you don't have to act on it.

"I'm proud to say that my husband and I made love for the first time on our wedding night. We also discovered that we are very sexually compatible, which wasn't a big surprise. Many people are afraid they will be stuck with a bad sex life if they abstain until marriage. But I truly believe that you can gain a very good idea as to what kind of lover a person will be just by the way he kisses you, touches you, and treats you. If you are attracted enough to the person to fall in love with him and you want to marry him, then I don't feel there will be a problem. Sexual compatibility is so much more *emotional* than *physical*. I believe meeting my mate had to do with "Divine Intervention" for me. I don't feel that I chose my husband. I believe he was sent to me. It may not work that way for everyone, but I believe it did for me. I had faith that we would be compatible.

"We feel good about having waited. We feel our relationship is truly blessed. We have peace in our hearts and in our relationship. We don't feel that we should have done things differently. On our honeymoon, we had totally clear consciences. It was exciting because we were experiencing something for the very first time together. Also, we both believed that if this person had enough self-control to refrain from sex and yet be that close, the chances of that person being faithful were much greater. This is a great feeling and makes our marriage much stronger. I also love how my husband appreciates me. One day he told me that he had never *made love* to a woman, except me. That showed me that he saw our lovemaking as very special. We're on a whole different level than what we were both used to before."

Marci

Marci had been single for a very long time and figured she might never meet the right person. "I met Neil through a friend. We talked for over six hours on our first date. He was different from all the other men I had dated. We dated nonsexually for about three months. He just didn't seem to be preoccupied with sex. I suppose he was more concerned with finding a true mate. Anyway, one day we were sitting in his parked car. He turned to me, put my face in his hands and said, 'Marci, will you marry me and be my wife for as long as we both shall live?' I was touched. This man made me feel so loved. He treated me more ten-

derly than I had ever experienced—and he still does!
I couldn't believe that he was willing to marry me
without having had sex with me. I was willing to go
further than we had gone but because he didn't push
it, neither did I. Boy am I glad I didn't. To know that
he loved me so deeply before we even made love has
made our relationship special. Today we are very happily married."

Maggie

"I have found that there is nothing more important
than keeping one's soul intact and maintaining integrity. I had a pattern of getting sexually involved with
men I worked for or with. I hate to admit it, but in
each of these situations I believed that by having sex, I
could further my career. I found the opposite was true.
Inevitably I lost the job, not to mention my reputation.
I burned many bridges. None of those men really
cared about me, they were using me as much as I used
them. I felt so helpless and empty. Of course in the beginning it seemed exciting. But heartache and pain was
the end result. Thankfully, I was able to see the futility
of my actions and I was finally able to break the pattern. I have discovered that when we live with integrity
and we are willing to forfeit short-term pleasure for
long-term well-being, we receive more opportunities
than we ever imagined. By living in harmony with
spiritual principles, we become blessed. We draw in
men who wouldn't think of questioning our morals or
trying to change our minds. Our talents become more
apparent and our purpose in life is revealed. We no
longer feel the need to sell ourselves short. We are
more free to fully be ourselves."

Freedom

My first experience with freedom came when I ran away from home at fourteen. I had so much anger bottled up inside. I was angry at my parents for not being the kind of parents I wanted them to be. I was unhappy and hated that my father wouldn't stop drinking. Why did he have to continue being that way? Why couldn't he just stop? I felt I had to get away. I had to break free from all the pressure, the control, the pain. I needed some peace. So I packed a duffel bag and left. It was in the middle of the night and I'll never forget the way I felt as I was walking down the street that chilly evening. It was like a huge weight had been lifted off my shoulders. I had never felt lighter. I could breathe. All the voices and the clanging in my head stopped. For the first time in a long while, everything was silent. I was free.

Although I'm not recommending that young people run away from home, I want to point out that abstinence has brought me a similar kind of freedom. I'm free to create the kind of relationship I've always wanted rather than settling for whatever I get. I'm free to choose how far I'll go with a man and I'm free to walk away when I know it's not right. I'm no longer a prisoner of my own emotions and my sexual desires. Freedom has come at a price but what is serenity worth? For me, it's definitely been worth the struggle.

6

Rebuilding Self-Esteem

In this chapter, we are going to look at a very sim-
plified process of rebuilding our self-esteem. I say *rebuild* because for most of us, through our childhoods
and our relationships, our self-esteem has been damaged in some way. We absolutely must work toward
having a higher level of self-esteem if we are going to
achieve happiness and make better choices in the
future.

A Look at Low Self-Esteem

Sometimes a person can appear to be very confident
yet suffer from low self-esteem. The following is a
brief description of how the malady manifests itself.

A person with low self-esteem is needy and unable
to say no when she doesn't feel comfortable in a situation. As it relates to sex, she may have sex with
men she's not in love with and possibly doesn't even
like. She operates from fear—fear of losing him, fear
of not being loved, fear of not being accepted, fear of

abandonment. A person with low self-esteem sub-consciously says, "I can't imagine being in a relation-ship where he completely adores me and tells me often how much he loves me. I've never had that and probably never will."

A person with low self-esteem is unable to be hon-est with herself. She has a difficult time seeing her re-lationships with others as they really are and instead finds ways of justifying her involvements. A person with low self-esteem blames others for her problems rather than taking responsibility.

A woman who sees herself as a victim usually has low self-esteem. And of course, a person who was abused as a child is a victim. But once that person reaches adulthood, they need to work through those feelings and rise above them.

Roseanne

"When I was a child, I didn't fit in at school. I was a complete outcast. Kids made fun of me. They wouldn't invite me to parties, and sometimes one or two girls waited to beat me up after school. I had no idea why all of this was happening to me. I tried to be nice. Maybe I was too nice. I don't know. I only know that it hurt tremendously. I wondered what was wrong with me. Why did everyone hate me so much?

"Then, I'd go home, which was also a hostile place. My father drank constantly. He and my mother fought late into the night. If I said one wrong word, my father would hit me and then tell me how stupid I was. He knew the problems I was having at school, but instead of helping me, he too called me names. He said that it must be my fault and that I probably wouldn't amount to much.

"All of these experiences created serious problems for me throughout my life. I never felt loved by others, so how could I love myself? I figured I just wasn't lovable. I saw myself as a big loser because it seemed everyone else did too. As a result of all this, I found myself avoiding doing things that I otherwise might have enjoyed. I didn't try out for cheerleader when I reached junior high. I didn't date the really sharp guys, instead I dated the ones who were considered trouble. I just didn't have the confidence. I thought for sure I'd fail at everything, so I gave up. I had a hard time looking people in the eyes. I was scared to death of practically everyone.

"Once I hit puberty, I became promiscuous. I guess I felt that was the only way to feel loved and accepted. I didn't feel I had anything else to offer. Those around me had convinced me of that. My self-esteem didn't improve with the sexual encounters. They only made it worse.

"Needless to say, I have a lot of work to do on myself. I definitely need to learn to love myself and actually believe that I am lovable. I think I'm finally open and ready to do just that. I'm tired of being afraid, insecure, and lonely."

Rosanne's story may be somewhat extreme, but it probably isn't as unusual as we might think. Many of us come from dysfunctional backgrounds, and all of us have experienced pain and humiliation at some point in our lives.

Now it's time to put all of this behind us and make a fresh start. We can rebuild and change the way we see ourselves and break unhealthy patterns.

A Look at High Self-Esteem

A person with high self-esteem feels worthy of love and commands respect simply because of how she feels about herself. She feels in control of her life and her relationships. No one is able to take advantage of her because she knows how to set limits and boundaries. She is in touch with her feelings. She knows when something doesn't feel right. When this happens, she quickly takes action in order to make the situation more appropriate. She stands up for herself when necessary. She makes sure her needs are met. She knows who she is and what she wants in life. She knows what her values are. She accepts herself as a woman who is growing. She strives to improve what she can, and she accepts that which she is unable to change. She is at peace with herself. She doesn't blame others for her problems. She knows that she is in control of her destiny.

A woman with high self-esteem is also willing to take more risks. She is able to walk away from a bad relationship even though she knows it will be painful. She is able to venture out on her own if that's the best thing for her to do. She looks for opportunities to improve herself and to live up to her full potential.

When we have high self-esteem, we become more interesting and desirable to others, especially men. We stand a little taller and smile a little brighter. We feel more whole and that's how we appear. Our body movements become more natural. We appear more relaxed and calm.

We all want to be around people who are confident and who seem at ease in almost every situation. We are drawn to those who are healthy and radiant. And

Why We Want to Have High Self-Esteem

A high level of self-esteem has many benefits. These include the following:

- You enjoy more peace of mind.
- You exude confidence and self-assurance.
- You make healthier decisions.
- You choose better partners.
- You attract better partners.
- You have the courage to say no to things that are harmful to you.
- You are able to say yes to the things that are good for you.
- You don't worry as much about what others think about you.
- You won't second-guess yourself as much.
- You are able to walk away from hurtful situations and people.
- You have a more positive and grateful attitude.
- You feel hopeful about your future and feel worthy of love, kindness, and blessings.

A journey of a thousand miles must begin with a single step.

—Lao-tzu

we are turned off by those who are needy, depressed, and empty.

I realize that this is a very simplistic view of self-esteem. Perhaps it seems unrealistic. But why make it complicated if it doesn't have to be? All the solutions in life are simple—it's the implementation that's difficult.

In the following two examples can you determine which woman possesses higher self-esteem?

> Paula: I have the worst luck when it comes to men. I attract all the jerks! They all seem to be interested in one thing, and I'm sick of it! I just wish I could meet a nice guy who wants to get married, but I seriously doubt there's any such person. The last boyfriend I had really took advantage of me. He lied to me constantly. Now, I wonder if I'll ever be able to trust anyone again.

> Candace: I know I've made some poor decisions in my life, but I've learned from them. I don't intend to make those same choices because I want something better for myself. I used to blame the men I was involved with, but now I know that I played a big part in the relationship. Now I'm in control.

Paula obviously has low self-esteem. But even Candace, although improving, still suffers from low self-esteem. We don't change our self-concept overnight. But the difference is, Candace is able and willing to be more honest with herself, and she is committed to change. Paula is still blaming others for her misfortune. She is choosing to remain a victim.

It's all in our attitude and in our willingness to do whatever it takes to change. High self-esteem, confidence, and inner peace require a lot of work to obtain. But the pay-off is well worth it.

Six Steps to Higher Self-Esteem

If we consistently incorporate these six steps in our life, we will have the confidence and inner fortitude to feel good about who we are.

Step 1: Be Honest with Ourselves

If we are unable or unwilling to be honest with ourselves about who we are and what is going on in our lives, then it's impossible to learn to accept ourselves and develop high self-esteem.

An important area to focus on is our feelings. When we're in pain, we need to acknowledge that we are in pain. If we are in pain because we had sex with someone and now he's not calling, then we need to acknowledge that feeling. What many women do is avoid the truth and blame it on something else. We may end up generalizing. We say things like, "What a creep! Men are all dogs. He was obviously afraid of commitment. I'm better off without him." Maybe this man did mislead you but that's not the point. The point is, in every situation, we need to be honest with ourselves as to what we are really feeling and why. A more honest comment might be, "I really wish I hadn't slept with him. I sort of lost my mind in the heat of the moment, and now I realize that it was just too soon. I'm feeling very hurt right now because he's not calling." It's healthy to acknowledge your feelings no matter what they are—but then we need to take responsibility. In the above scenario, her concern shouldn't be why he didn't call, but rather why she chose to sleep with him so soon. Being honest allows us to get to the heart of the problem.

When we acknowledge the truth, we can then learn from our mistakes and begin to make the necessary changes to get on the right track. We can come up with some new behaviors that will work for us and not against us. But if we continue to blame the situation on others or justify our behavior, then we become stuck.

Changing negative patterns requires taking a good look at our past relationships and the most effective way of doing that is by putting it all down on paper. We can't know the solutions until we know what the problems are or have been. As difficult as this was for me, it was the best thing I ever did for myself. What a revelation it was for me to see on paper my history of the past seventeen years! I was able to gain a better understanding of my relationships and my approach to the sexual part of those relationships. I learned what my true motives were and what I was feeling. At the time I may have been in denial or unaware of these feelings, but today I can see them more accurately.

I have dated some wonderful men. Without knowing them, I would not be who I am today. I am very grateful for my past experiences because of what they've taught me. Sometimes we have to make mistakes that hurt us in order to learn what we need to learn. Sometimes reading a book that has all the answers just isn't enough, and we have to go out and skin our knees a little. We do not have to be ashamed of our past experiences, we only need to learn from them. Almost all schools of psychology teach that mental health is based upon being honest with ourselves and becoming aware of our feelings and emotions. One definition of insanity is doing the same things over and over, hoping to get different results. We no longer have to do this.

Creating Your Relationship History Chart

Making a Relationship History Chart is a powerful exercise we can use to see the patterns in our relationships.

In a notebook or journal, draw lines down a page to make several columns. At the top of each column, write the name of every man you have had a relationship with. Below each name, write your age at the time of the relationship and a brief description of the nature of your involvement. Write down how you became sexually involved and why you chose to do so at the time. What was going through your mind? What kind of discussion did you have prior to being physical? In some cases, you may not have had intercourse, but any form of foreplay where you bonded emotionally should be included. Then, under that write out what your *true* feelings are about the situation. Be honest and try not to get into your head too much. Just stick with your feelings.

Even if you are a virgin, completing a Relationship History Chart is beneficial. There are plenty of women who are technically virgins (no intercourse) yet who have a sexual history.

The chart on the next page is an example of a Relationship History Chart. We can see how Sally's sexual behavior changed over the years. She made the decision to be sexual for many reasons. Once, she was very depressed, unemployed, down and out. Another time, she was lonely and in need of some companionship. Seeing these reasons helped her to see the problem more clearly. She saw her part in the process. She could see that in order to avoid falling into sexual, dead-end relationships, she had to improve her self-esteem and develop her own happiness and fulfillment

Sally's Relationship History Chart

Nathan	Andrew	Alan	Patrick
19 yrs old. Met at a party. Had sex on first date. Had no discussion about the future. Continued to date for about 6 months.	23 yrs. old. Wanted to do it right this time. Did not rush into sex. Discussed commitment beforehand. He told me that he loved me. After one year we broke up because we fought too much and it wasn't leading to marriage.	25 yrs. old. I was at a low in my life. Very depressed, unemployed. Just wanted someone around. He was there, we were friends at first, so we had that bond. I wouldn't have sex with him for the longest time. We did discuss being monogamous and we did express loving feelings for each other before having sex.	Present: 28 yrs. old. Fell in love before we even kissed. Do not have a sexual relationship (I already made the decision to abstain), so the relationship is not based on sex. We are talking marriage.
→			
I had sex with him essentially because I didn't know how to say no! I thought I had to, and I guess I wanted to feel wanted by someone. I really felt that I loved him, but now I know it wasn't true love at all.	I loved him, but I still felt something was missing. Even though he said he loved me, he did not want to marry me and that hurt (even though I had my doubts about him). I didn't wait long enough because our commitment wasn't strong enough. Felt like I lost a part of myself.	Because we made a commitment before having sex, and because I knew I did not want to marry Alan, I did not have those horrible feelings of being used. But I did have the emptiness because the relationship wasn't based on love and there was no future. Total lack of fulfillment and a real sadness. Also, something wasn't right. I was in it for the wrong reasons.	Finally, I feel completely loved, adored, cherished. He truly respects me and my values. Feel extremely secure within the relationship. If we had had sex, I believe the relationship would have continued with the same loving feelings, but I would have felt badly because of my spiritual beliefs. I know that his feelings are sincere and not about sex, even though he is a very sexual person. I have finally learned that building love has nothing to do with sex and I finally know what

as well as determine her values. Also, her values changed over the years. As she experienced the pain of having sex too soon, she intuitively knew to try new behavior in the next relationship. As she finally made the decision to be abstinent, she was able to experience a deeper kind of love. She finally got what she had wanted all along but not just because she met the "right" guy. She achieved a deeper kind of love because of her own efforts to change.

By making our own Relationship History Chart, we may see that we chose to bond sexually and emotionally with men who were not right for us. We may discover that we knew that right from the start, but we chose to ignore the truth for various reasons. When I did my own chart, I saw that most of my decisions relating to sex had been a contradiction of my true inner values. I had been living in opposition to my spiritual beliefs. Many of the women I interviewed admitted that for years they chose to have sex with men who did not love them and who they didn't love in return. They explained that this is why many of them had to be drunk or had to invent elaborate rationalizations. Many had to be "swept away" in order to make it seem like it wasn't their choice—and ultimately not their fault. When we behave in this way, we aren't being true to ourselves. And that's what has to change.

❖❖❖

Sylvia is a woman who has everything going for her by all outward appearances. She is very attractive, dresses smartly, and has a great personality. She never has a hard time getting a date. But Sylvia continually gets involved with men who don't treat her right. They make plans with her only to cancel at the last minute. Her latest boyfriend, Darryl, sometimes even forgot about the plans they had made. He often called late at night wanting her to come over. Because of her neediness, she usually accepted the invitations.

Sylvia would call her girlfriends and go over every detail of an evening with Darryl. She would go on and on about how mean and inconsiderate he was to her. One night he threw her out of his house angrily because she had expressed frustration over his seeing someone else. She was hurt and couldn't understand why all this was happening to her. She couldn't figure out why Darryl was so loving and interested in her one minute and abusive the next.

Sylvia had a difficult time seeing that her problems were of her own making. True, Darryl was not a healthy person either, but Sylvia was inviting the abuse by making herself available to it. She *knew* Darryl was an abusive person. She knew he was seeing someone else. She knew that he wasn't emotionally available for a healthy relationship. Yet, she continued to call him and accept his invitations to get together.

Sylvia is unable to be honest with herself about her situation. She still wants to blame Darryl. Self-honesty is the first step in her breaking free from her situation.

Step 2: Eliminate the Negatives from Our Lives

We can't grow if there is something in our lives that stunts us. That something could be drugs, alcohol, a person, unhealthy eating patterns, an addictive relationship, or anything else that is holding us back from achieving happiness. Growth then becomes a matter of letting go, eliminating, or leaving behind what is holding us back. It's when we *resist* letting go that the real pain increases. When we hold on to something that is obviously causing us pain, our self-esteem inevitably suffers.

We need to decide what to accept as a part of our lives and what not to accept. When we say good-bye to unhealthy relationships or "situations," then the growth process can begin. But we need a clean slate in order to begin the journey.

Life is a process of letting go. We begin by letting go of the warmth and security of our mother's womb and making our way into the world. We let go of crawling, of our baby teeth, of the security of staying home when we reach kindergarten age. In adulthood we might have to let go of friends, family, or jobs to pursue new opportunities. We have to see this letting go as positive. It may be difficult to let go, but ultimately, we make it harder on ourselves if we do *not* let go.

Think back on your life and bring to mind all of the things you have let go. Now, think about how well you handled each situation. You obviously survived the ordeal. Of course, losing a friend or relative to death is more difficult than losing your favorite shirt. But even with death, we miraculously seem able to recover. It's when we are going through it that it seems so hard. Just remember: *This too shall pass.* Nothing will last forever.

Many of you reading this are in a relationship that you know you must let go of if you want to grow. You're holding on partly because the pain you know you will experience frightens you more than the idea of staying. I will explore this in more depth in chapter 8, but for now, begin to muster the courage to follow your conscience. Only then will your self-esteem be free to grow.

Step 3: Self-Acceptance Is the Key

Most of us find some aspect of ourselves to dislike. We think our noses are too big, or we're too short or too fat or not educated enough. Very few people are completely satisfied with everything about themselves, and if they were, we would think they were arrogant. Even people with high self-esteem dislike certain things about themselves. Yet, people with high self-esteem do something about the traits they are able to change. And they accept the traits they can't change.

Most of us who have suffered from low self-esteem are familiar with feeling inadequate. We think we only we need to be rich or beautiful or successful. Maybe our parents gave us the clear message that we were inadequate. But now we are adults, and we need to be our own parents. Remember, we are through with being a victim.

Others form their opinions of us based on the messages we send out. People will pick up on our feelings of inadequacy and treat us accordingly. But if we can overcome those feelings and develop inner confidence and a feeling of self-worth, then others will pick up on that, and the treatment we receive will improve. It's all up to us and what we think about ourselves.

I remember the days when I felt so insecure about my looks I was miserable. I hated my chin because I thought it was too long. I couldn't stand my profile because I felt my chin was more obvious from the side so I did everything in my power not to let people see my profile. You can imagine what a challenge that was! I'm surprised I was able to carry on a conversation considering how obsessed I was about my chin. Well, as my self-esteem grew and I learned to accept myself more, I began to relax. Now, I just let it all hang out and the interesting thing is, no one really notices how long my chin is. And as my father always said, "Laurie, people are too concerned with *themselves* to worry about you or anyone else!"

Accepting Being Single

We must accept that we are single and be comfortable with it until the right man comes along. If we are incapable of doing that, then we will end up getting seriously involved with the wrong men just to fill a void and end the loneliness. We need to enjoy our own company and not rely on relationships with men to make us feel okay about ourselves.

I don't think we can just wake up one day and say, "From now on, I am going to enjoy being alone!" A more subtle process must take place within ourselves. And that process begins by becoming aware of what we are attempting to do and by trying to obtain it. When we end a relationship, we need to sit ourselves down and have a talk. We need to tell ourselves that we are not going to get into another relationship immediately, rather we are going to do nice things for ourselves. We are going to cook ourselves special dinners and read lots of books. We are going to go to movies alone and plan other activities. And we are actually going to learn to enjoy ourselves, even *like* ourselves! Basically, we are going to have a relationship with ourselves, and it is going to be a wonderful experience. It is going to be a relationship that lasts forever and becomes stronger with time. We will eventually have a relationship with a man, but through it all, we will also have ourselves.

While we need to learn to like ourselves and enjoy our own company, we also need to be of service. True happiness does not come from a self-centered life. It comes from getting out of ourselves and serving others. This should always be a priority.

Step 4: Embark on a Spiritual Process

The beginning of practically any spiritual process is simply accepting that there is a power greater than ourselves that we cannot see but that greatly influences our lives. A spiritual person is one who accepts this force and shows respect for it. Years ago, when I lacked faith in the idea of God as my creator, this is how I began my spiritual process. I realized that I couldn't possibly be the most powerful force in the universe, so I developed a small amount of faith in what I called, "The Spirit of the Universe." I knew there was a power much greater than myself, but that was the extent to which I believed at the time. Over the years, my spirituality has grown by leaps and bounds. Today, I believe in a loving God who has answered every one of my prayers, healed many of my inner wounds, and transformed my life. I have learned that spiritual growth comes when we are humble and open. Many want to create their own idea of what is true or spiritual. But I believe that true spiritual growth comes from being open to the guidance of the Spirit. When we humbly ask for wisdom and truth, we will be led to it. If, on the other hand, we want to construct our own belief system based on what is convenient or least challenging, then we aren't really being receptive. We can't be led to where we really need to be. All that is required to begin a spiritual journey is a willingness to believe.

Beginning a spiritual process will be different for everyone and might include the following. (This list is not meant to be complete.)

- Praying and meditating daily
- Going to church
- Reading spiritual books
- Surrounding yourself with spiritually-centered people
- Seeing a therapist (although I don't necessarily see this as spiritual as much as psychological, many people have grown in a spiritual sense as a result of therapy. By talking things through with a professional they were better able to understand their patterns and thus became more open for growth.)

As you pray and ask for guidance, you will be led to the right path for you. Search out spiritual answers. You can find the truth and allow it to heal your soul and fill the void you may be experiencing.

Other important aspects of growing spiritually have to do with making promises to ourselves. They include the following:

Making Amends.   As we are honest with ourselves and able to own up to our mistakes, we can see the damage we have done to ourselves and to others. We need to make a list of those people we have harmed. We should approach them, if possible, and let them know we are sorry. Their response is irrelevant. We are simply taking responsibility for our wrong actions. It doesn't matter if they did more harm to us. We are only cleaning up our side of the street. As we do this, our self-esteem will grow tremendously. We will feel more at peace with ourselves than ever before. We will be free from the guilt and resentments that have been holding us back.

Completing a Relationship History Chart.   The more aware we are of our patterns, the easier it is to arrive at solutions and make a change. Healing comes when we are being honest with ourselves about our past.

Making a Personal Pledge.   We will discuss this in the following chapter. This is extremely important because once we make a pledge to ourselves, we have a very clear standard by which to live. We no longer have to doubt where we're coming from or wonder how to handle a situation.

Gaining Support from Other Women.   We all need the help and support of others as we strive to live in accordance with the standards we set. Being true to ourselves is no easy task. Being able to turn to other women who know what we are going through makes it a lot easier. I have been fortunate enough to develop friendships with many wonderful women, all of whom have touched my life in various ways. As we laugh together, cry together, and allow ourselves to become vulnerable together, we develop a bond that is unbreakable. The women in my life have taught me much about love, unselfishness, and compassion. Without a support system, it can be difficult to grow spiritually. We need to share our pain and frustrations with those who understand. Reach out to the women in your life. God has a way of putting the right people in our paths when we need them. Some of our friends will be those who help *us*, and others are the ones *we* help. But one thing is for sure—we definitely need each other.

Ready for Change

When we are ready for change, the answers appear. Anytime I have needed to make a radical change in my life, it has come about as a result of turning to God. I have had three major turning points in my life, and they were all brought about by my willingness to surrender.

The process for me has been very simple. It typically begins with my becoming sick and tired of living my life in a way that is causing me a lot of pain. I get on my knees and humbly ask God to help me. He does. It is that simple. He has helped me by sending people to me who have the right answers by leading me to a particular book that contains the answers I need or by slowly changing me and helping me grow from within. He can do the same for you.

Step 5: Avoid Situations That Undermine Self-Esteem

Putting ourselves in situations that undermine our self-esteem is obviously going to damage our self-concept. Being in an abusive relationship or one that is lacking in love and tenderness are prime examples. When we remain in these types of relationships, we begin to develop resentments and guilt. We slowly begin to hate ourselves because we know we are living a lie. We are not being true to ourselves; we have been ignoring the voice that tells us to get out of the situation.

There are many other ways we damage our self-esteem. If, for example, you don't do well at large-group events and you find your self-esteem being negatively affected, then simply stop going to these events. Perhaps in the future, as your self-concept improves and you develop the skills you now may lack, you can attempt a large-group gathering again.

But why should we continue to put ourselves in situations that we find painful or debilitating? If we find that a certain friend criticizes us, there's nothing wrong with ending the relationship, at least for awhile. We need to avoid situations that tear down all of the rebuilding we are doing.

Step 6: Create New Standards for Ourselves

High self-esteem comes from doing what is right. As Dr. Laura Schlessinger writes in her book *Ten Stupid Things Women Do to Mess Up Their Lives*, high self-esteem is earned. When we live in accordance with our values, we begin to feel good about ourselves and our self-concept improves. We have integrity and we become more confident. When we go against our values, our self-esteem drops. We begin to feel poorly about ourselves, and it shows.

As I have mentioned earlier, we need to listen to the still, small voice inside us. It takes practice to recognize this voice, but if you ask yourself, "What does my heart tell me to do?" The answers will come. You will feel a peaceful clarity about the situation.

As we set new standards for ourselves, we become clear as to what we will or will not accept in our lives. This could mean not allowing another person to abuse us ever again. It could mean never allowing

ourselves to get involved with men we know are unhealthy or emotionally unavailable. We begin practic-
ing new behaviors. This could mean not calling him
anymore or saying no when he asks to see us.

We are all at different stages of growth. When we
first begin the process of setting our standards, we are
taking baby steps. For example, start by setting a goal
of not calling him for one week or even one day. If you
are trying to end a sexual relationship but find yourself having a difficult time, you could make a pledge
to not have sex for one week. Then, when the week
ends, renew your pledge for one more week. As time
goes on, you will begin the withdrawal process and
eventually you will become stronger. The key is, you
have to want to change more than anything else. And
that takes action.

As our self-esteem grows, not only will we like ourselves better, but we'll begin to feel more worthy of a
high-quality man who will cherish us. Our low self-
esteem may have been what led us to having sex too
soon in the past. Now it's time for our *internal voice* to
decide for each of us when the time is right. Once we
have looked inside our hearts, we are in a position to
think of abstinence from sex as a way of achieving
love.

7

Deciding When to Have Sex

In our past relationships, how often did we actually make a *conscious decision* to have sex with our mate? I am talking about making a rational, mature decision based on our feelings, his feelings for us, a discussion of the future, and the nature of the relationship right at that time.

We usually jump into sex blindly without much consideration for these issues. It is extremely difficult to be rational, logical, and mature when our mind goes on temporary leave. But rationality is exactly what we need to make these decisions *ahead of time*, when all of our clothes are on, and, preferably, when we are alone rather than in his arms or affected by his powers of persuasion.

Isn't This Being Unromantic?

I looked up the words "romance" and "romantic" in the dictionary. Romance is defined as a strong, usually *short-lived* attachment or enthusiasm. For romantic, I found two definitions of interest: "(1) Imaginative, but impractical and (2) Not based on fact; *imaginary*." (Italics added.)

Let's take a good look at our Relationship History Chart, and see if some of our past sexual encounters resemble these definitions. Haven't some of our encounters been very strong and passionate in the beginning, yet ultimately *short-lived*? Even though both parties became caught up in the romance and sex happened naturally, now that it is years later, don't you feel that it was at least partly based on fantasy?

Romance is great if it means doing loving, thoughtful things for each other in order to enhance the relationship. But when it comes to something as serious and powerful as sex, we need to make sure that our practical side participates in the decision-making process.

We Set the Standard

Men are capable of setting the sexual standard in a relationship, but it is usually the woman who decides *when* sex is going to happen.

Maybe a non-sexually aggressive male sounds pretty good to you, especially if you just had a date with a guy who resembled the Tasmanian devil. But most of us would not like it for long. After the fifth date, we would look at him and say, "Don't you find me attractive, or what?" We would begin to think something was wrong with us. We would do everything in our power to get him to notice us. If that didn't work, we would lose interest.

The fact is, we like men just the way they are, even though some might find it excruciatingly painful to admit it. Oh, it might be nice if men were not quite so intense about sex. Maybe. But we would go a little crazy if they were not all that interested.

Taking Inventory

Up until this point, we have been contemplating and observing our past relationships. We know that having sex too soon is dangerous and won't get us what we want. We have been looking at the state of our self-esteem and trying to understand men. It's as though we have been out to sea and have dropped anchor for awhile to observe the vast waters, the weather, and sky. We have taken inventory of our supplies and determined what needs to go and what can be salvaged. Now it is time to pull in the anchor, determine our course, and set sail. It is time to make *the* decision to determine our actions and direction.

The Course We Choose May Change with Time

Even though I always have felt deep down inside that sex outside of marriage was wrong for me, it has taken me years to accept this. At times I took on other points of view. At one point I felt that just being in a committed relationship was enough. However, over time, I always came back to my original belief. Such fluctuation can be seen by some as wishy-washy, and indeed, sometimes it was. But we all go through a process in life where we learn from our experiences, our pain, our joy, our failures, and our successes. We learn what works and what doesn't. Only then can we adjust our actions accordingly.

Today we may choose one standard but as we journey through life, we will determine that a different standard suits us better. We should not choose a standard based on what others think we should do. We know what to do. The answers are all right there, within our heart. Our heart will direct us, and our heart will help us create a stronger, clearer-minded, joyous woman.

The Three Standards

Study these three standards. Spend some time pondering what each one means and how you feel about it. Consider your religion, your upbringing, your feelings, your past experiences, and your goals. Don't worry about society or how men or others will react. This is just for you. We are going to discuss briefly what each standard means, the pros and cons of each, and how to address these issues before getting physical.

Standard 1: Requiring a Commitment

With a commitment, both persons verbally agree not to date other people. You also verbally agree that the direction of the relationship is *marriage*. This must be very clear. Many misunderstandings have occurred simply because the exact terms of the commitment were not spelled out clearly enough. Both persons should understand that the relationship may not end up in marriage (you are willing to take that risk), but marriage should be the goal.

For your own peace of mind and happiness, if you choose this standard, you will want to make sure that neither of you are going against religious or moral beliefs by engaging in premarital sex.

Pros

- You weed out the men who are not serious about you, or who are not ready for a real relationship.

- You gain a clear, verbal understanding of where the relationship is going.
- You feel more secure.
- You create an opportunity to establish a foundation of love.

Before making a commitment, you should have determined the following:

- You trust him.
- You love each other and express it verbally.
- You spend adequate time together.
- Your relationship goals are the same.

Cons

- Either of you could change your mind, which could cause a lot of pain.

- Commitment does not always mean the same thing to everyone. Misunderstandings can and do occur.

- Both of you may rush into making a commitment, possibly so that you can get close physically. Later, you may find that it was a mistake.

- You still run the risks of getting pregnant or contracting sexually transmitted diseases.

- You can remain stuck at this point. Men often become comfortable and are less motivated to go to the next level of commitment.

A Sample Conversation

Prior to physical contact, you should engage your partner in an honest discussion of your need for prior commitment. (The ideal time for this conversation is when he makes a sexual advance.)

YOU: *I'm not interested in being in a sexual relationship unless we are completely committed to each other and are headed toward marriage. I need to know what kind of relationship you want to have, and what your feelings are for me.*

HIM: *I know I have very strong feelings for you, and I do want to have a relationship. I'm not sure about marriage, because it is just too soon to tell.*

YOU: *I have made the mistake in the past of getting sexually involved too soon. Not only did it affect me negatively, but it hurt the relationship. I do not want to make that same mistake again, so I would prefer to wait until we are both clear that we are actually in love and that we are working toward marriage. We just aren't ready to be sexual.*

Note: Once you have made this decision and have verbalized it to him, stick with it! If he quickly agrees to a commitment, you know it is probably an impulsive decision. It would be a good idea to wait and see how sincere he is. Discuss your feelings for each other, marriage as the goal, and a time frame. If you still don't feel completely comfortable, continue seeing him, watch his actions, and *go with your intuition!*

Standard 2: Requiring Formal Engagement

Under this standard, you do not have sex until you are formally engaged—with a ring and a wedding date set.

Pros

- You know he is sincere and committed.
- Love precedes sex, which means the relationship is more solid.
- A stronger, deeper commitment has been made.

Cons

- Engagements can be broken.
- Men have been known to propose only with the intent of getting the woman in bed.
- The relationship can become stagnant. He may be less motivated to get married.

A Sample Conversation

This is an example of the kind of conversation you need to have if you require a formal engagement prior to having sex.

YOU: *I happen to take sex very seriously, and although I do not feel the need to wait until I am married, I do plan to wait until I am engaged. I just do not want to be sexually involved with someone again until I know I am going to spend the rest of my life with that person.*

HIM: *I am not into casual sex either, but to wait until we are engaged could take a long time!*

YOU: *I agree, but it shouldn't take us an enormous length of time. Most people know fairly early in the relationship whether or not they could marry that person. I just don't want sex to get in the way of us being able to discover our true feelings.*

Some women think it's pushy to talk about an engagement when they've just begun dating. But remember, men usually have no problem making sexual advances, so why should you have a problem ensuring that your needs are met? Besides, you are not proposing to this man, you are simply stating that you are not available for a sexual relationship outside of being engaged to be married. Let him know you're in no hurry. The ball is in his court at that point.

Standard 3: Requiring Marriage

Under this standard, you do not have sex until you are legally married.

Pros

- You have both made a total commitment.
- You feel no risk of being used or taken for granted.
- You create the space for true love to grow.
- You are not preoccupied with sex.
- You do not have to worry about getting pregnant or contracting diseases (if you are free from disease beforehand).
- You know his intentions are sincere.
- You know he loves you completely for you and not just sex.
- The relationship moves at a more natural pace rather than becoming stagnant.

Cons

- You run the risk of being sexually incompatible (although there are ways of determining compatibility without having sex).

- You likely will suffer, as you do when you deny yourself just about anything!
- You may lose a few men along the way (though they'd be men who will not accept your standards, which could be a blessing).

A Sample Conversation

This is an example of the kind of conversation you need to have if you do not believe in sex before marriage.

YOU: *I feel that sex is a very sacred, special act that should be shared between two people who are married. Although I'm not a virgin, my values have changed. It is very important for me to be with a man who can accept my feelings about this. My religious beliefs mean a lot to me.*

HIM: *I do feel very strongly about you, but I can't say that I am ready to propose marriage. That takes a long time to determine, and I'm not sure how we can have a relationship for that long without having sex as a part of it. Besides, since you are not a virgin, I feel like somewhat of a fool to wait when you haven't in the past.*

YOU: *I know this may be new for you, but it means a lot to me. I realize that we are a long way from considering marriage. The very reason that I am asking you to respect my wishes on this is because I see you as a very special person. Time will tell if we should be together forever. Although these were not always my values, they are my values today. For me, sex outside of marriage is wrong. I hope that you will be willing to continue in the relationship, but if not, I understand.*

I think it's pretty obvious that Standard 3 is the safest choice that will give you the most security. I also believe that waiting to have sex until we marry will bring us the deepest love. I realize this seems unrealistic in today's world, but believe me, it isn't. You would be surprised at how many people actually are waiting until marriage. The couples I spoke with who had waited, seemed to have the best marriages. You don't necessarily have to have religious reasons for waiting until marriage, although most people do—anyone can choose this standard.

Important Issues to Consider Prior to Being Physical

Regardless of which standard you choose, important issues must be discussed before being physical. We will cover how to get a commitment in the next chapter, but you will need to talk about these issues when he makes sexual advances or when the discussion comes up.

How You Feel About Him. Since women usually determine their feelings quicker than men in relationships, most women will already know if there is potential by the time he makes advances. Yet, many women become so obsessed with getting *him* to commit that they forget about considering if they even want to be exclusive themselves. Ask yourself these questions: Are you in love with him (or at least "falling" in love)? Have you talked about compatibility issues (see chapter 13)? Would you want to marry this man and have his children?

How He Feels About You. A man should express his true feelings for you before he makes any sort of sexual advances. But unfortunately, many men don't. They just "go for it," because it is much easier than sorting out their feelings, which can be very uncomfortable for them. This is unacceptable, and you need to let him know this. He needs to know that you would never consider being sexual with someone who does not love you and who hasn't discussed the nature of the relationship first or with whom you are not married. Do not ask him directly if he loves you, just give him the opportunity to express his feelings in his own time. No matter what he tells you, take some time to ponder what your intuition tells you.

The Amount of Time You Spend Together. The amount of time you both spend together that you feel is adequate is a very individual matter. Some men will say they want a serious relationship, yet they only want to get together once a week, which makes for a very lonely relationship. It also makes you wonder how sincere he really is.

A common scenario is that you spend a lot of time together in the beginning, but shortly thereafter the time together becomes less and less. On the other hand, there are many couples who do not spend very much time together and are perfectly happy with the arrangement and are committed to each other.

The key is to determine what is acceptable for *you.* Do not ask him directly how much time he plans on spending with you. He probably won't know the answer anyway. Watch his actions and see how he behaves naturally. If he wants to make time to be together, he will. You may already feel very secure in this area because he is calling you every day or every other day, and you are together a lot. But these things are subject to change. Watch for consistency.

The Future.   This is probably the most crucial area to consider because no matter how strongly you feel about him or how much time you spend together, if you are thinking marriage and he is not, you've got a problem. You are stuck in a relationship that becomes stagnant. You are both at a stalemate and you are usually the one who gets the worse deal. So before being sexual, you should discuss the future and his intentions. More than anything, watch his actions. We intuitively know from our inner voice if a man is really serious about us. The way he treats us usually makes it obvious.

If you choose Standard 1, and you have made your commitments, then establish a time—say, several months to a year—when you will both sit down and discuss moving on to the next level (engagement). The same applies if you are choosing Standard 2. If you both agree on a time limit, then you avoid having the relationship drag on forever.

Length of Time You Have Been Together.   You could date someone for six months and have a lesser degree of love and commitment than a couple who has been together for only six weeks. Although it rarely happens, there are couples who meet and fall deeply in love almost immediately. You can cover a lot of ground in a short period of time and determine that you want the same things in life and that you are ready for a serious relationship. I do believe, however, that to fully get to know someone takes time. So although the feelings may seem strong and everything seems like a go, the longer you take to fully get to know each other, the better. I suggest one year.

How to Tell If He Is Being Honest

Unfortunately, there are men who will say whatever it takes to have sex with you. It's hard to believe anyone would do this, but it happens all the time. Some men clearly are just out for one thing. Others may make a commitment to be exclusive with every intention of keeping that commitment only to discover that their feelings have changed. It happens, and it's a risk you take when you have premarital sex. Attend to a few key warning signs:

- He only wants to come over or wants you to come over to his place.

- He is very touchy right away (puts his hands on your waist, touches your hair a lot, etc.).

- He makes very aggressive physical advances right away (within the first couple dates).

- He asks very personal questions relating to sex, very early in the relationship.

- He tries to change your views about sex, attempting to convince you that you are wrong.

- He is constantly staring at your breasts or other personal areas.

- He does not seem interested in getting to know *you*.

- He strongly encourages you to drink or take drugs.

If you suspect that he is only interested in sex, then telling him you are not available is the wisest thing to do. He may change his ways down the road, but I wouldn't stick around to find out. I think it's better to find a man whose priorities are different. *Taking your time* and being *very observant* can help prevent you from going too far with a man who's only interested in one thing.

Making a Pledge

Many of us have had sex with men we don't like, love, or even know very well. Now it's time to make a pledge to ourselves as to what our standard will be from now on. When we make a formal pledge like this, we take the decision more seriously and we have a starting point from which to begin our new life. After making your pledge and sticking to it, you will begin to feel empowered, joyful, and excited about your future.

Personal Pledge

From this day forward, I will not have sex until I am committed, engaged, or married (choose one). From this moment on, I am taking full control of my body.

8

Getting a Commitment

Not all men are commitment-phobic. In fact, I believe very few men are actually *afraid* of commitment. They only avoid commitment when they are not sure of their feelings for the woman or if they feel pressured into making a commitment. Men want love and even marriage, just as we do. At times they might be a little more skittish of the idea than we are, but that doesn't mean they won't eventually commit. After all, look at how many men are married!

Unfortunately, many men will avoid commitment if they are able to have a sexual relationship without one. They have become spoiled in this regard. They know there are plenty of women out there who will engage in casual sex, therefore why make a commitment? In order to have *you*, though, more is required. Any man who wants you badly enough will have to give you what you need, and most will do so gladly. And besides, many men are getting tired of being able to obtain sex so easily. They *want* a woman of virtue.

Many women think they somehow have to make a commitment happen, when all they have to do is have faith in the process. A man will go to the ends of the earth and do whatever it takes to make a woman his partner in life once he finds a woman who captures his heart. Men will actually *ask for a commitment from you* when they want you badly enough.

Quite often a man will make a commitment once he knows that casual sex isn't possible. When you say no to sex, he is put in a position where he must consider how he feels about you. He says to himself, "Hmmm . . . she won't let me have sex with her . . . so, do I see a potential future with this woman? How much do I want to invest here? Is it worth it to me?" He'll wrestle with this for awhile so be patient. I know this is difficult to do, but it's the only sane choice you have. This is where most women get into trouble. They get fearful that they have lost him or that they came on too strong with their requirements, they doubt their position, and then they call him. This can give him the idea that perhaps she wasn't completely serious. He thinks that maybe her mind can be changed.

You have nothing to gain by calling him or by compromising. Give him time and space to determine his feelings. He needs to digest what you have told him and what is required in order to have a relationship with you. Believe me, you want him to be completely clear and resolved about this decision.

If he decides to enter into a serious relationship with you, you'll be glad you were patient because once he makes that decision, the falling in love process has begun. He is now invested and fully willing to build a relationship. Congratulations! You now have the beginnings of what might be a beautiful, lasting relationship.

The emphasis here is on *beginnings*. You're not at the altar yet. But don't worry, you're well on your way. You have the tools to make it happen. What you need to do now is continue to feed the fire and build upon the foundation you have begun to establish. You are deepening his feelings for you.

To awaken these powerful feelings of love in the man of your choice, there are certain rules that should be followed, especially in the very early stages of a relationship. Most of us don't like rules. But as I have found out from experience, these rules absolutely work. They make the relationship better and help build a strong foundation. I know of several exceptions to these rules, but they are vastly outnumbered.

Five Basic Rules for Dating

Rule 1: Don't Call Him

Women often ignore this rule and yet they can't understand why men stop pursuing them. How can he pursue you if you are pursuing him? There are many ways to justify calling, but doing so isn't in our best interests.

We end up calling him out of fear, insecurity, and impatience. We become frustrated when he doesn't call, and we want to know how he feels about us. But if we are secure about ourselves and the relationship, we will be relaxed. We know he will call.

A man must have time to think about you and then decide on his own that he must talk to you. Some women are afraid that men won't be aggressive enough about relationships, so they try to make things happen. If he is interested in you, he will call. If he doesn't call, it won't do you or the relationship any good if you call him. It only creates an awkward situation that you will regret, and it frustrates the pursuit for him. There is a time when it's okay to call him, but I suggest you wait until it's established that you are a couple or are returning his call.

One definition of pursue is "To follow in an effort to overtake or capture; chase." If you are *not* pursuing, you have an attitude that says you don't want anything, whether it's a date, a commitment, or even a phone call. This attitude gives a man plenty of space for his own feelings to develop and triggers his interest in you. If you aren't pursuing him, then he will naturally take on that role, which is what you want. Allow him to chase you until you catch him!

In *Getting to "I Do,"* Dr. Pat Allen cautions that it might take up to eight weeks for a man to finally call. Anything beyond that time and you should give up hope of him calling. From my own experience, I can say she's right. Eight weeks can seem like an eternity, but if you keep busy and be patient, it will pay off. (It usually doesn't take eight weeks for him to call, anyway.)

There are many reasons why a man may not call right away, and they usually have very little to do with you. Don't take it personally.

A man I used to work with met a woman he really liked, and they began dating. He told me he needed to call her that day, as he told her he would. He was looking forward to setting up another date. As the day progressed, I asked him if he had called her and he said, "No." He just hadn't gotten around to it. At the end of the day, he still hadn't called her, although he said he still planned to. I couldn't understand his approach and I asked him, "How can you put off calling her all day like this? Aren't you excited about talking to her?" He looked perplexed and replied, "Oh, of course I am, but I've just been busy doing other things. I'll get around to it though."

This is just one of the differences in how men and women behave in relationships. For us, the relationship is much more important than whatever tasks have to be done. Most of us would have called as soon as we could. But the important point here is, he wasn't *not* interested in her. Quite the contrary. He was just moving at his own pace.

Rule 2: Don't Be Physically Aggressive

As we've already discussed, refraining from being physical, especially at the start of a relationship, is very important. At this point you probably already know that you want to avoid being sexual. But you also want to be careful not to be too aggressive in other physical ways. This includes putting your arm around him or reaching for his hand.

Being physically aggressive is another way of putting yourself in the "pursuer" role. This might backfire and scare men away. They may feel pressured. They might assume you are more interested in them than they are in you. Although this rule is not etched in stone, being a little reserved is much more mysterious and attractive to men.

Rule 3: Allow Him to Lead

Letting him lead means sitting back and allowing him to give what he wants to give and do what he wants to do, without constantly fighting him or his ideas. When I say allow a man to lead, I am not suggesting that you never voice your opinions or desires. I'm not talking about being totally submissive. Men don't always want to be the decision-makers. They appreciate a woman who has opinions and desires of her own. But they also don't appreciate a woman who is overly pushy and who doesn't allow them to lead. There is a balance and an art to getting this right. Remember, the longer you are together, the more of a team you become. But in the first phase of the relationship, it's important to let him lead.

When you let him lead, he feels as though you trust him and his judgment. You also give him the feeling that you are happy to just be with him. A man loves knowing that being with him is all that really matters to you. It will be easy to let him lead if you are really interested in him and if you are compatible.

My ex-boyfriend and I had some problems when we were dating, so we decided to see a therapist for some guidance. She asked us what the problem was. He said, "We fight too much. It seems that we're always locking horns." The therapist suggested we do something that I never would have expected. She suggested that for two weeks I had to say yes to whatever he wanted to do and go wherever he wanted to go (unless it was immoral or unethical) with absolutely no fight, argument, or attitude. I was not to call him at all, but he could call me.

She could see that I wasn't allowing him to lead and that I was fighting him and trying to control him as well as the relationship. So her advice was to go to the other extreme, temporarily at least, in order to see the benefits of doing so, and to take the pressure off my boyfriend.

Well, I did it and I have to say, it was one of the best experiments I've ever conducted. I didn't call him or initiate getting together. I allowed him to make all the decisions. If he asked me what I'd like to do, I told him, but I didn't try to control the time we spent together. The result? His entire attitude and treatment of me transformed. I felt so much more loved. We didn't argue once. He wanted to spend more time with me than ever before, and we got along beautifully. I didn't feel at all that I was compromising or doing things I really didn't want to do. Even though our relationship ultimately did not work out due to other incompatibilities, I learned a very valuable lesson that I will carry with me always.

Rule 4: Keep Him Guessing

It's important not to wear your heart on your sleeve. Don't let him know how you feel about him—at least not until he expresses his feelings first. You want to share your love for him in layers, a little bit at a time.

Not being too available is another way of keeping him guessing. Let's look at Molly's experience. Molly always felt that if two people were meant to be together, things would just work out. Her motto was, "Just be yourself and don't hold back."

She finally met a man, Cameron, whom she felt was real marriage-material. She was elated. He seemed to like her also, although she wasn't sure to what extent. But he did ask her out and continued to call.

Whenever Cameron called, Molly was right there by the phone. She usually kept her schedule open just in case he asked her out, and if she did have plans when he wanted to see her, she quickly canceled them. When he came to pick her up, she rushed to the door with waited anticipation and her exuberance was obvious. So what happened? Molly isn't sure, she only knows that Cameron doesn't call as often as he did when they first met. He seems to have lost interest. The more he pulled away, the more she chased him and the more desperate she appeared—until Cameron lost all interest.

If Molly would have just contained her emotions *temporarily* and become more involved in her own life, she would have been more interesting and challenging to Cameron. It isn't that she would have been playing games, she would simply be cautious and smart. She wouldn't have been dishonest. She would have been behaving in an intelligent, mature way.

Rule 5: Don't Oversell Yourself

Pointing out all the great things he should know about you can make you seem as though you are trying to sell yourself. You have the appearance of being insecure or desperate, and it isn't very appealing. But you don't have to prove anything.

When we meet a man in whom we're really interested, we want to make a great impression and let him know what a great catch we are. We want to subtly reveal the fact that we're a great cook or graduated with honors. But the mistake we sometimes make is we overdo it. If we draw all the attention to ourselves, we may succeed in impressing him and gaining respect, but we won't make a love connection.

A much more effective approach is to look for things *in him* to be impressed by. Who you are will be revealed to him slowly over time until he is convinced that you are the perfect woman for him. But in the beginning, find out all you can about him. You are looking for things *in him* to appreciate. You are also deciding whether or not he's for you.

It's much more intriguing to a man when a woman's personality, character, and soul unfold *slowly* over the course of an entire life-long relationship. The more he discovers about you, the more impressed and fascinated he will become. Don't make the mistake of blurting out your entire life story on the first date or even the first few dates. Especially don't talk about ex-lovers or past sexual experiences.

By the way, when a man asks you how many lovers you've had (this is my least favorite question—right up there with "Can I borrow some money?"), tell him it's really none of his business and that it's a very inappropriate question. He's setting you up to either pass or fail, and I don't know about you, but I don't like to play games. It just isn't a fair question. If it really didn't matter to him, he wouldn't ask. But it does matter to him and therefore the answer, regardless of what it is, is going to affect him. We aren't obligated to reveal this kind of information and if he's a gentleman, he'll back off when you express your feelings.

Just like us, men want to feel as though they have found someone of great worth. They want a woman in whom they can feel extremely proud. Remember this: A woman who knows her worth doesn't feel the need to overtly prove it. She will subtly let him see her wonderful traits, but she doesn't obviously bring attention to them. Most important, when you know you are a woman of great worth, your relationship will continue to grow.

Following these rules will make a dramatic difference in how aggressively he pursues you. Throughout the relationship, whenever you are feeling as though you are giving too much, you can use these concepts to bring the relationship (and his feelings), back into balance.

Be Interested in Your Own Life

A man wants to know that you enjoy your life, and that you have your own interests and are not just looking to attach yourself to the first man who comes along. He doesn't want to be a target or an escape for a woman who is simply bored or in need of a financial provider. It's important to be your own person and have a full life, independent of your relationship with a man. This also will keep you from being overly vulnerable to his charms. When he sees your joy in living, he will want to commit.

When You Don't Know His True Feelings

Nothing is more frustrating than not being able to tell what he is thinking and feeling, especially if you are crazy about him! The good news is, he will eventually express his feelings. He'll have to. He will get to the point where he feels he has no other choice but to tell you that he loves you. Do not ask him. Don't seem concerned. That would inhibit him and make him feel pressured. All you need to do is be patient.

Trust in the process. Remember that inner voice that is guiding your heart. Everything must take its course. It's much more intriguing if he can't figure out what *your* true feelings are. A word of caution, however: Do not use intrigue as a way to torture a man. This should never be done.

When He's Dating Other Women

Until a man makes up his mind that he wants to be exclusive with you and makes the commitment to do so, he is free to date other women. This is partly out of your control because even if you get him to commit and he is not really ready or willing, the commitment won't be very solid. He eventually may end up dating other women anyway if that's what he really wants. We can't control people.

Also, don't bring his dating up or try to talk him out of it or seem overly concerned. What you can do, however, is continue fulfilling your part of awakening feelings of love with him (see chapter 14) until he comes to the conclusion on his own that you are the only woman he wants.

I dated a man who said he really wanted to be able to date other women. (Our relationship was non-sexual.) My old self would have been angry or felt rejected. He clearly would have known how unhappy I was with the situation. I even might have accused him of being noncommittal. My new self said "Fine." I didn't worry about it. I didn't worry because I knew he would come around. I knew that he would get over his desire to date other women. I had confidence in myself and in our relationship. I simply continued to be the kind of woman who captured his heart in the first place, and I continued doing the things that got him interested in me from the beginning. Sure enough, one night over dinner he told me he had lost all interest in seeing other women and all he could think about was me!

If He Won't Commit

If he just won't commit, it could mean one of the following:

He Knows You Aren't the One for Him.   He may change his mind on this later, but for now he is not convinced that he wants something serious with you. Even if you have become physical with each other, he may secretly know you aren't right for him. He may not let on that this is the case, especially if he wants to continue being sexual. If you are sure that you want him, apply all of the principles in this book. If you're having sex, stop. Completely start over and see if he doesn't come around. Most men do.

You Didn't Set the Right Standard at the Start of the Relationship.   If you don't set the right standard up front, it's a constant battle trying to regain control. If sex occurs too soon, it's almost guaranteed that his feelings will be altered. Getting a true commitment becomes more difficult. A strong foundation wasn't created, therefore the relationship is on shaky ground. The only solution is to start over by ending the sex and setting a new standard. We will discuss exactly how to do this in the next chapter.

He Is Not Sufficiently in Love.   If he is unwilling to commit, then his feelings aren't deep enough. You will have to set a new standard and continue applying all of the principles in this book in order to deepen his feelings. Study chapters 12, 13, and 14 to determine the areas you need to work on the most.

It Has Nothing to Do with You.   Perhaps this man is incapable of committing to anyone. Maybe the timing is bad for him and he won't allow himself to fall in love. But remember: Love has a way of changing a man's mind, no matter how stubborn he may have been before.

What Not to Do When Trying to Get a Commitment

Here is what to avoid during this process:

Asking for a Commitment Directly.   A man has to *want* to be committed to you. If you verbally ask for one, then you have become the pursuer and you might scare him away or turn him off. *Remember that he will give what he wants to give based on how he feels, not based on what you ask for.* Focus on deepening the bond between you, rather than asking for more.

Hinting.   Hinting can backfire. He knows what you are after and so the effect is the same as asking directly. He will feel like you are after him, which automatically puts him on the defensive. He feels backed up against the wall, rather than motivated to more aggressively pursue you.

Demanding a Commitment. This will rarely get you what you want. Commitment should be the man's idea—or at least he'll want to feel it is—so when he feels you demand one, it's no longer his idea. It's forced upon him. Nothing will drive a man away quicker.

9

Ending a Sexual Relationship— Or at Least Ending the Sex and Starting Over

$\mathcal{D}$eciding to abstain from sex is obviously much easier if you are not currently in a relationship. You can establish your standards, make a Personal Pledge, and then when you do become involved with someone, you are completely prepared. You know what your boundaries are and you know how to deal with the various responses you might receive from a man. But your life may be a bit more complicated. You may be in a relationship where you no longer feel comfortable having sex, yet you don't necessarily want to end the relationship. Or, perhaps you want to end the relationship completely. You may even be in a sexually addictive relationship that is creating a lot of pain for you.

Breaking Up

Breaking up is horrendously painful. It's similar to the feeling you get when someone you love very much passes away. You know you aren't going to be seeing that person anymore and, in a way, you are losing a part of yourself. We invest so much of ourselves in relationships.

Breaking up is usually more painful when our relationship is sexual (and it lasted longer than a few weeks). If you haven't had sex with him, you're not as emotionally bonded to him and walking away is much easier. You don't feel as though a part of your soul is lost. Knowing that a little sadness now is better than a lifetime of being with the wrong person will help you make it through this difficult time. Remember that the pain eventually subsides. It's important to allow yourself time to heal, so that you will be available for the right man.

If you know that breaking up is the answer, then just *do it*. Don't waste precious time. Don't continue to allow yourself to be in an unhappy or unhealthy situation. Make a clean break. Change your phone number if you have to. Move to a new location or avoid going where he goes. Get him out of your system and regain your balance. One day you will look back and wonder what you ever saw in him.

A Word of Advice: When breaking up, don't mislead a man. If you honestly don't want to see him anymore, then come right out and tell him so—and then stick with it. I know how hard breaking up is. You usually end up back together at least three times before the relationship actually is over. But along the way, at least be honest about your feelings.

Starting Over—Yet Remaining in the Relationship

Ending the sex in a relationship yet trying to stay together is one of the most difficult things a person can ever do. We ask a lot of ourselves when we try to remain in a love relationship, without sex, with someone we have had sex with before. If two people know that they want to get married and they have plans to do so, then staying together without having sex probably will work. All that's required is some self-control and common sense (and a lot of cold showers). It may be more difficult for him (he might try to convince you of that), especially if he doesn't have the same values you do. If he really loves you and plans on spending the rest of his life with you, then he'll be willing to wait if it's that important to you.

If you don't have plans to marry and you're not anywhere close to getting engaged, then you've got problems. You are two people gratifying your sexual appetites while you drift along aimlessly. The only solution is to move away quickly. Today's fun can be tomorrow's sadness and heartache.

How to Start Over

If you are in a relationship with a man and you want to continue seeing him but you just don't want to have sex anymore—at least until you are either engaged or married—then what you need to do is very simple. You begin by being direct. Say something like, "Joe, I really care about you, but I've come to the conclusion that I don't feel comfortable being in a sexual relationship. I would like to continue seeing you but only if we can do so without sex. I have decided that

I am going to wait until I'm (engaged, married, or until we are more deeply committed) before I get sexually involved again. It has nothing to do with you, it only has to do with how I feel. I'm just not happy this way and so I'm making a change. I hope you can accept this because it is very important to me." You can use your own words and style of communicating, but don't be wishy-washy.

To be able to say something like this and actually mean it is not the easiest thing to do. But even more difficult is sticking with the decision. Remember your Personal Pledge. I have found that the pain of remaining in a relationship that causes us to go against our values is a lot worse and lasts much longer than letting go of the relationship.

Separating *temporarily* is another option. This creates an opportunity for the two of you to have a regrouping period whereby you can each gain clarity and inner strength. When you do reunite, you are better able to begin with a clean slate. Another benefit of a temporary separation is that the intense emotional bond that was initially created by the two of you having sex loses some of its intensity. You can then set a new standard, one that feels right to you.

Once he has been told of your intention to stop having sex, a man may react in a number of ways:

He May Not Take You Seriously, and He Will Try to Change Your Mind. As I have said before, we need to make the decision as to when we actually will say yes rather than allowing ourselves to be talked into sex. Saying no and yet having sex makes us a victim. Choosing when we are going to be physical and not allowing anyone to change our minds puts us in control. Stick with your decision.

He May Feel a Need to Distance Himself.   Once a man has had sex with a woman, it's very difficult to just stop the sex. It may be difficult for us, too, but it's probably easier on us because abstinence was our idea. Not having sex any longer can bring us peace of mind whereas it can bring him a lot of frustration, depending on his belief system.

Give him the space he needs. Don't panic and think that you have got to do something. He will work it out and, most of the time, he will come to terms with the situation. Depending on how strong his feelings are for you, he may prefer remaining in the relationship. Let him pout. It will add to his growth.

He May Express Confusion.   Since sex affects men differently, it only makes sense that they won't fully understand your reasons for wanting to abstain. They may be confused about what to do. They don't know what to think. The best way to deal with this problem is to honestly express your feelings and reasons for wanting to wait. If he still acts as if he is confused, don't let him use this as a technique to change your mind. After awhile, his understanding is not your concern.

He May Feel You Are Playing Games with Him. Make it very clear that your reason for the change is so that *you* can feel good about *yourself.* You are not giving him an ultimatum. Only an inconsiderate man would become angry after such an explanation. We need to do our best to educate men about how we feel when it comes to sex because most of them honestly don't understand what we experience. But keep in mind that they may never understand.

The Inconsiderate Man's Response

There are all kinds of men out there at various levels of spiritual growth. In this section, my intent is simply to point out the difference between a considerate, caring response to your desire to stop having sex and a selfish, inconsiderate response. Remember, even the nicest guy may have trouble with this in the beginning. But an inconsiderate man will consistently respond in one or more of the following ways:

- He will not be concerned with your feelings.
- He will be more concerned that he won't be having sex.
- He will continue to put pressure on you to have sex.
- He will not listen to what you have to say; he will only try to convince you that you are wrong, silly, and immature.
- He will not be interested in finding out what *you* need in order to feel more secure.
- He will drastically distance himself from you or simply disappear with no discussion or closure.

Here are responses some women have heard when declaring their desire for abstinence:

I used to get so angry with John. I kept telling him my reasons for wanting to abstain, and he said he understood. But he continued to try to get me into bed. Many times I would give in. He saw the pain I was going through and he saw how depressed I became, but he kept doing it again and again. I was mad at him for days. He could never understand why I was so angry. I told him it's like walking out in the street and getting hit by the same bus every day and each time the bus driver continues to try to convince me to walk out in front of him! After awhile, I'm going to get angry with the driver, even though it's essentially my fault for doing it!

◇◇◇

It's as though all of my words went right out the window. I told him I just couldn't continue having a sexual relationship, and yet, even as the words were coming out of my mouth, he would be all over me, trying to get sexual.

◇◇◇

When I told Jerry that I felt we had sex too soon and that I wanted to start over without sex, he came unglued. He accused me of being crazy and childish. He said it didn't make sense given that I'm not a virgin. I felt like all he really cared about was sex.

The Considerate Man's Response

- He'll say he understands. The last thing he wants to do is hurt you.
- He'll let you know that your relationship is more important than sex. If you need more time, it's okay with him.
- He will wait until you are ready.
- He asks what will make you feel more comfortable or more secure.
- He will not run away just because you aren't having sex.

It is refreshing to have a man actually listen to you as you explain how you feel, and then have him lovingly tell you that he understands and wants to do whatever makes you comfortable. Now that's a guy we all could marry! He's the kind of guy who will be there for us when we are old and gray, or when we are ill or ten pounds overweight after having the baby. Life is too short to spend our time with men who basically don't care about our feelings. Don't make the mistake of thinking that men will help you remain abstinent. Even though they might respect your values, if you're willing to yield, they'll usually take the opportunity to have sex. Accept this and take full responsibility for your own actions.

We need to be able to recognize a good man and avoid the rest. We can get a good idea of what kind of man he is when the discussion of sex comes up. Remember, a man is much more open to discussing having a nonsexual relationship when he loves and respects you. If you don't get the response you are hoping you will get, then he will probably not be the one who will see you through your reorienting yourself to the love-first-and-sex-later way of living.

10

Responding to His Advances Without Bruising His Ego

Wʜen it comes to sex, men can be very persuasive. "Come on, let's just lie down together. We don't have to do anything!" They may be denied gracefully a few times in the beginning of a relationship but at some point, they will resort to every line, gimmick, plea, or protest known to women.

If you have made the decision not to have sex until you are in a committed, monogamous relationship or are married, then you will want to be prepared with some strong comebacks just in case. It isn't that we are protecting ourselves from *men*, it's our *decision* not to have sex too soon that we are protecting.

Some men are so polite that you may wonder if they're even attracted to you! Some men assure us that they'll wait until we're ready (as they glance at their watch). And, more and more, men are the ones who insist on waiting until a stronger bond of love has developed (I personally like it better when it's *my* idea). No matter what type of man you are dealing with, it's best to be prepared. There is always a certain amount of expectation of sex in a relationship but you set the standard.

It may be awkward to discuss your sexual values on the first date or even on the first few dates. For example, don't start the evening off with, "I won't have sex until I'm married." It may put him off. In fact, I wouldn't be surprised if he says he wants to call it a night very shortly after you share that information. It's best to wait until the man makes some sort of advance or until a serious discussion is initiated. If he's not trying anything, why bring it up? He may not have had any intentions of getting physical with you; thus, you may appear presumptuous, overly paranoid, or as though you are, as a friend of mine puts it, "craving his carcass." Men sometimes assume that if you bring the subject of sex up—in whatever context—you must be interested and are potentially open to sex.

Instead, just focus on getting to know him. Most likely, it won't be long before he'll raise the issue of sex. At this time, as we discussed in chapter 7, you can simply say that you take sex very seriously and that you are not interested in getting that close with someone until the time is right. If he wants to know when that might be, then be honest. Remember, the good ones stick around.

When the subject comes up, just be matter-of-fact about your beliefs, no matter how much he may chide you for being old-fashioned. Don't act embarrassed or be defensive. Be proud of your standards. Be light-hearted, joyful, and carefree. The men you date will have such a good time with you that that's what they'll remember.

Being Sensitive Without Being a Pushover

Men are extremely sensitive when it comes to their sexuality, and we need to be sensitive to them. It isn't our responsibility to *satisfy* their sexual desires, but

there are ways we can be considerate. These suggestions will typically apply only after the relationship
has developed somewhat. They are useful when you
know that you are interested enough to hang in there,
in spite of not being sure if he's "the one."

1. *Put yourself in his shoes.* Always be considerate
   as to how he might be feeling. The man you are
   with has feelings for you. He has a strong desire
   to express those feelings and get close to you.
   Remember, he is only reacting to the way he
   feels, and he usually feels that making an advance is the right and natural thing to do.

      We can really make men endure a lot in this
   area. On one hand, we want him to pursue us, and
   on the other hand, if he doesn't try anything, we
   get hurt and upset and then wonder if he's even attracted to us. So do your best to explain your feelings, and then when he respects your wishes, be
   appreciative. Don't give him mixed messages.

2. *Appreciate his attraction to you.* Take it as a compliment that he is physically attracted to you
   and wants to make you feel good. Tell him that
   you are attracted to him too (if you are). Don't
   take his attraction to you for granted or act like
   it's expected.

3. *Let him know it's not personal.* A man usually
   takes rejection personally, which can seriously
   affect his pride. Assure him that it's only because
   of your need to do what's right for *you,* and not
   because of something unappealing about *him.*

4. *Be firm.* While you are considerate and understanding, you also must be firm about your convictions. You should not feel sorry for him, and

you are not responsible for making it all better. You definitely are not going to have sex with him to relieve the tension that he might be experiencing! He needs to know that you mean what you say, which will only deepen his respect for you. This firmness must be obvious to him from the very beginning, and he must not see you questioning your own resolve.

Convincing Him That You're Not Frigid: Forget It!

It is not your responsibility to *prove* that you are not frigid. All that you are obligated to do is assure him that you are perfectly normal in this regard (if it's true). Sometimes when you tell a man that you don't want to have sex until you know each other better, what he hears is, "I don't like sex, I'm not into it, so don't even think about trying!" But that's not what we're saying. Say to him, "Look, I am a sexual person, and there is nothing wrong with me. I don't have any particular hang-ups that would alarm you. You will have to trust me on this."

Keep it light and quickly change the subject. If he's persistent about discussing it, you could simply say that you don't feel comfortable discussing such intimate things so early in the relationship. Let him know that when you are comfortable, you will share more with him. This will likely stop him cold.

The Lines Men Use

Sometimes men act as though their entire lives depended on sexual contact! "Can I just take a peek? Just *one* look? Let me just touch once, *pleeease!*"

All we can do is set our standard and see how he responds. Men love challenges, and when a woman sets sexual boundaries, most men are going to try everything they possibly can to break through them. It's within their nature. We shouldn't criticize them for it. Obviously, men were created this way for a reason and we should be grateful that they have this drive. Otherwise, men wouldn't pursue us as aggressively, and we probably wouldn't ever get married and procreate!

We also can't blame men when we end up giving in to them. We've got to take responsibility for our own actions and realize that no one can make us do anything. Don't allow men to control who you are and what your values will be.

When a woman who has been in a sexual relationship for a time brings up commitment or marriage, a man might say something like, "It's just too soon to know! We've only been dating nine months (sixteen years or whatever length of time)!" The logic goes, "It *isn't* too soon to have intercourse—the most intimate act there is—yet *it is* too soon to know how serious you want to be with a person." We know something is wrong here. And it's up to us to end this destructive trend.

Here are some of the lines men commonly use and some suggested responses for them. You will need to adjust the wording, depending on whether you want to wait until you are committed, engaged, or married.

LINE: "We won't do anything, I just want to hold you (or kiss you)."

RESPONSE: "I would love to get close to you, but I just don't want to put ourselves in a dangerous situation."

LINE: "Let's just watch a movie at my place. I've had a hard day and I don't want to go out."

RESPONSE: "I'd rather not be alone at your place. I just don't feel comfortable with that." (If he persists, you can suggest getting together another time.)

LINE: "I feel like I'm back in high school! We're adults here. I've never met a woman your age who feels this way!"

RESPONSE: "I'm not saying we have to wait until we're married. I just don't want to become sexual with someone until I know that we have established the intimacy that deep love brings. Doesn't that make sense to you? After all, don't you want a relationship that is real and that lasts? Let's not ruin this right off the bat just because of our hormones."

LINE: "Why can't we just see what happens, play it by ear and let it progress naturally? This isn't a business, you know."

RESPONSE: "I agree, we should let the relationship progress naturally. We can take as long as we have to. I'm in no rush. But for me, sex is only possible once I'm in a committed, monogamous relationship. That's nonnegotiable."

LINE: "But I love you."

RESPONSE: "If you really love me, then you'll respect my feelings when it comes to this. If our love is real and it lasts, then there will be plenty of time for us to express that love physically." (If you don't want to wait until you're married and he tells you that he loves you, then you'll need to determine what your feelings for him are. If you love him too, then you'll want to discuss commitment—for example, Are you exclusive? Are you headed toward marriage? Have you established the closeness and the intimacy that "I love you" implies?)

LINE: "But sex is a natural part of a relationship."

RESPONSE: "I agree, it's a natural part of a *committed* relationship, and we are not fully committed to each other at this point. I don't want us to rush into a commitment, but I'm also unwilling to rush into sex."

LINE: "But I *am* committed to you!"

RESPONSE: "What does that mean to you?" (Let him explain. If he means that he only wants to see you and that he's in love with you, then at that point you need to determine if marriage is the goal and set a time limit. Then you need to listen to your inner voice to determine if it really feels right.)

LINE: "But even marriage isn't a guarantee."

RESPONSE: "True, but it is the highest level of commitment two people can make. It's the only commitment honored legally and the only one that would make me feel secure enough to give of myself sexually."

LINE: "I'm a very sexual guy, there's no way I can't be physical."

RESPONSE: "I understand how difficult it must be for you, it is for me too." (Remember to be understanding even if he is not.) "However, I can't go against my feelings. I'd rather miss out on the temporary satisfaction I'd get by having sex now than miss out on the possibility of building a solid, lasting relationship." (You'll need to be confident enough to say that maybe you aren't the right woman for him if he persists.)

LINE: "I'm just so attracted to you, I can't help myself. You drive me crazy."

RESPONSE: "I'm attracted to you too, but we're going to have to exert some self-discipline because it will only destroy our relationship. We shouldn't just react to our physical drives. We have the ability to control our bodies and not let them control us."

LINE: "But this is the '90s, everyone is doing it!"

RESPONSE: "I know everyone is *not* doing it, but even if they were, it doesn't matter to me. It just doesn't feel right to me and I will not compromise my values. We are not just everyone else. We are special together."

LINE: "If you really loved me, you would do it."

RESPONSE: "Do what? Ruin the specialness of our relationship? I feel that if you really loved me, you wouldn't pressure me to do something that I don't want to do." (You need to convey the message that you care about *yourself,* which he should respect.)

LINE: "If you're not going to do it, then I'll get it somewhere else!"

RESPONSE: "Good luck. Don't let the door hit you on the way out!"

LINE: "Your views are just too old-fashioned and outdated."

RESPONSE: "I'm sorry you feel that way. They feel right to me. I'm sure there are plenty of women out there who will go along with your way, but I'm not

one of them. I would hope you would see abstinence as a way for our love to grow."

LINE: "But you've already done it before, so what's
the difference?"

RESPONSE: "I have a different set of values today
and I've got to be true to them. I believe a person
can start over anytime and that's what I've chosen
to do. Besides, I would hope that you might want
to be part of a new, more evolved relationship."

LINE: "There's no way I could marry someone
without knowing what she is like sexually."

RESPONSE: "I can see how you would feel that way.
I realize it's scary but if two people truly love each
other and communicate their emotions, I know
they can create a beautiful sex life in a marriage."
(Again, you must be willing to say you may not be
the right woman for him rather than try to persuade him to see things your way.)

ANOTHER RESPONSE MIGHT BE: "I agree that sex is
an important part of a marriage but if two people
love and respect each other, sex isn't going to make
or break the relationship. You work at creating a
wonderful sex life."

LINE: "How do I know you're not frigid and that
you are a sexual person?"

RESPONSE: "I believe you can easily see that I am a
very affectionate, warm person. If I had any hang-
ups, or lack of desire, I would tell you. Besides, our
chemistry speaks for itself."

LINE: "How will we know if we're compatible
sexually?"

RESPONSE: "There are ways of finding out compatibility: By talking about our sexuality—our level of desire, what feels good to us, and what doesn't feel good. We can tell if we're compatible by our kisses and touch. If we truly love each other and are physically attracted to each other, then chances are we will be compatible. We have got to have faith that we can work things out no matter what and that we can make our sex life great if we want to."

LINE: "It's unnatural to suppress your sexual urges."

RESPONSE: "No one has ever died from not having sex, and besides, it's only temporary. Although we may strongly *desire* to have sex, we don't necessarily *need* to have sex in order to survive."

Main Points to Remember

Men Can't Argue With Your Feelings.   They could try, but it's foolish and they usually give up. Your feelings are your feelings. It helps tremendously if you remain focused on them in your conversations with men as they try to get you to compromise. What can a man say when you say over and over that it just doesn't *feel* right? He may not fully understand you, but he'll have to respect your feelings. If he doesn't, he's not the kind of man you'd ultimately be happy with anyway. Don't allow it to turn into a fight. The bottom line is, he either respects your feelings or he doesn't. If he doesn't, let him go.

You Must Come From a Confident, Strong Place.   To use the responses mentioned above, you have to be confident. You've got to stand firmly behind what you say. If you allow him to talk you out of your position, then it appears that your values don't mean anything to you. You've got to believe in your standard and speak from strength.

You Must Be Willing To Lose Him.   This can be extremely difficult: If you really love him, the last thing you want to do is risk losing him. But only when you are confident enough to take that risk will you be able to get the attention of a good man who appreciates and respects your standards. Being desperate never works in any situation. You don't want to try to talk him into seeing things your way or agreeing with you. It's up to him to accept or reject your standards. He either will come around, or he will disappear. Chances are he will come back. He may go out with other women who don't share your same standards only to become even more clear that you are the woman for him. If he stays, it is because of a respect for your values. It's also the beginning of a deeper love between the two of you.

Do Not Be Deceived by Feelings and Expressions of Love.   If you both truly love each other and have made a solid commitment—and have no problem with premarital sex—then you might feel ready for a more physical relationship. A word of caution: Feelings can change! It really hurts when you finally open up to someone who claims to be head over heels only to find out that he was confused, didn't really mean it, or was just in it for the challenge. (Watch out for the shrewd ones.) He may have meant it at the time but later realized that it wasn't a lasting feeling. When he is tenderly caressing you or is telling you how much he adores you and wants you forever, it is easy to give in. This is another reason why it's wise to wait until marriage.

H.A.L.T.   Alcoholics Anonymous uses this acronym, which reminds us *never to be Hungry, Angry, Lonely, or Tired.* When we become depressed or extremely disappointed, then we are more vulnerable. Our defenses are down when we feel these emotions and, thus, we need to be on alert to protect ourselves.

Love and marriage are going to be a part of your future, and it will be with a man who respects your feelings. Don't ever lose sight of that. It will happen if you have faith and overcome the obstacles along the way. You must be willing to lose a lot of men who could not or would not accept your standards. Remember: *Good things come to those who wait.*

11

Foreplay: How Far Can You Go Without Giving In?

Foreplay is defined as "sexual stimulation preceding sexual intercourse." Essentially, foreplay *prepares* us for intercourse. So we should ask ourselves this question: "If I'm not planning on having intercourse, *why am I preparing myself for it?*" A male friend of mine answered this question by saying, "We're just having an appetizer to see if the chef can cook!" But it isn't that simple.

Many women feel that if they refrain from *intercourse,* men will respect them. They rationalize the other sexual activity by thinking that as long as they don't go all the way, their reputation is preserved. Not true. Every man I spoke with did not see a big difference between petting and intercourse from the standpoint of a woman's virtue. Although this may seem like a double standard, the fact is, we shouldn't kid ourselves into thinking that men see us as virtuous simply because we are not having sex.

So why would we set ourselves up for the inevitable if that really isn't what we want? I think for the same reason that people smoke even though they know it's bad for them. Or why people overeat when they are supposed to be on a diet. We don't always do what we know is best for us—especially when it comes to our basic needs, desires, and pleasures. We try, but we don't always succeed.

Foreplay sneaks up on you—just like gaining those last seven pounds out of nowhere. You sure enjoyed yourself along the way, but now you step on the scale and say, "What *happened*?!"

We may start out a relationship with every intention of keeping it light—perhaps just a little kissing, but before we know it, we are in way too deep. Turning back is extremely difficult. The only solution is to determine ahead of time, with a deep resolve, how far you are willing to go and to avoid compromising situations.

This can be difficult because we want to connect with our mate. We want to merge and feel the bliss of kissing and caressing. It seems so harmless and actually, depending on your level of self-control and clarity of standards, it can be harmless. You will need to look at your track record. Have you consistently been able to avoid crossing the line you set for yourself? Or, have you failed miserably eight out of ten times?

Most couples alone in a romantic setting find themselves powerless. Why put yourself in this kind of situation? I believe we need to change the way we date. There's no reason for us to be alone in a house or apartment with someone we are just getting to know. I asked an eighty-year-old woman how couples were able to wait until marriage in her day. She told me, "Well, we went out on our date, and then he would take the girl home and say good-night. It was simple. We didn't spend lots of hours alone with each other in our homes. We went out, had fun, and just dated." So, what's wrong with that? Too unrealistic? I don't think so. Just because our dating habits have been drastically different for the past several decades, doesn't mean they have to remain that way. Again, it's up to us to set the standard. Whenever a man suggests you spend time alone at his or your place, you simply can say, "I would feel more comfortable if we went out or went for a walk." If he persists in knowing why you don't want to be alone, say, "I just don't feel comfortable with being alone at this point. I'd rather just have fun and get to know you better." He may have had no intentions of making sexual advances, but that's not the point. When we are alone in a secluded place, we create an opportunity for things to happen. I'm not saying that you can *never* be alone. Let your intuition tell you if a situation is okay.

The hard part comes when he begins to think you are uptight. But don't be fooled by what he means by "uptight." A male friend of mine was telling me about a woman he was romantically interested in who wasn't receptive to his sexual advances. He called her "uptight." I said, "She seems smart to me." And he replied, "Same thing." His comment was very interesting and revealing. Men know that the smart ones won't do anything they don't want to do. They know they're not afraid to say no to anything, even if it means being labeled *uptight.*

At issue is our level of resolve. How badly do we want to wait until it's right? How important is this for us? How strongly do we want a relationship that lasts a lifetime and is based on true love? If we enter into a relationship with the attitude of "We'd *like* to wait, but you never know about these things" then the chances are that we won't wait for very long. When we have determination, we create an unwavering resolve within that dictates how we are going to conduct ourselves. *Nothing* is going to cause us to compromise. By being true to our commitment, we benefit greatly.

But how do we feel when we compromise and lower our standards? As one woman put it, "Whenever I've gone too far, inevitably I feel remorse. I guess I also feel a certain amount of hopelessness, because I think I'm never going to get it together." Another woman said, "I don't feel as confident when I cross the line that I've set for myself. It's as though I've lost a part of me, so I don't feel whole and complete. I also don't feel as energetic and playful, because I'm more serious and heavy with worries."

Katrina chose to abstain until she was engaged. She "kept regressing," in her words, with an ex-boyfriend. I asked her to explain how she felt before and after her "regressions."

> I had been abstinent for several months and was feeling better than ever. I felt spiritually centered, happy, carefree. I noticed I was more lighthearted and less cynical.
>
> The problem came when I started spending more and more time with an old boyfriend, with whom I had at one time been sexual. At first we had no intentions of being physical, but over time I could see things were changing. It all started with sexual talk. We talked about what it used to be like for us, and what our sexual fantasies were. It was all very subtle and extremely seductive. We just slowly became more and more physical, until we ended up doing it all.
>
> So how do I feel now? Well, this morning I woke up feeling very unmotivated to start my day. I just stayed under my covers, looking around my room

for what seemed like hours, staring into space. When I think about what happened, it hurts. I made a promise to myself that I wouldn't have sex until I'm with the man I want to be with forever and I broke that promise. So today I feel terribly sad. There's an emptiness. I feel sort of detached from the rest of the world. I just want to go into my own little cocoon and avoid reality.

The problem comes if we try to convince ourselves that we are comfortable with certain forms of foreplay when we're not. We may be shut off from our true feelings, possibly as a way to cope. Patty is a woman who has given serious thought to these issues in her own life:

I suppose I justified heavy petting because I felt I was being so good by not having intercourse. But the feelings I experienced were almost the same. I felt unclean in a way. I still felt as though I had lost a part of myself. It took me several days to shake these dark feelings.

If We Get Started, We Probably Won't Be Able to Stop

Foreplay is like eating a piece of pie when you're on a diet. You tell yourself you're only going to have a couple bites, just enough to satisfy your craving. But you end up eating the whole slice. Likewise, one of the most obvious dangers of heavy kissing and/or petting is that once we start, we probably won't be able to stop.

When we participate in heavy foreplay, we disable ourselves in a sense. We become powerless, crippled by our lust for more. We lose the advantage of our logical mind, because we end up doing that which we clearly didn't want to do before. Then we pay the emotional consequences: Guilt, fear, self-loathing, despair. We doubt our self-worth, and our dignity feels crippled. Sometimes we start over. Other times we mask over the pain and ignore our feelings.

Bonding Through Foreplay

We become emotionally bonded when we engage in foreplay just as we do through intercourse. Some women may experience this to a lesser degree, but for many, there's no difference between foreplay and sex in this regard. Many times the bonding is even stronger since there is an unspoken closeness as a result of not moving too fast. Tammy is one of these women:

> I was dating someone who, without a doubt, was not right for me. We both knew it wouldn't work and, therefore, we decided not to have sex. We did, however, play around a lot. I was able to justify what I was doing, because we weren't doing "it." This sounds like high-school stuff, but I was thirty-six, and he was in his forties! He told me often how much he respected me and admired my strength. He felt our relationship was really special. I must admit that since we set some boundaries, our relationship did become stronger than all of my past relationships. I began feeling much more emotionally attached to him, even though we were only participating in foreplay. I wanted more, not only more of a commitment but more physical contact. I would ask myself why I set the boundaries in the first place. I would try to justify somehow giving up those boundaries so I could do it anyway. I played games in my head, but I always came to the same conclusion: *We just aren't right for*

> ## Where Will You Draw the Line?
>
> This book offers choices. Just as you must choose for yourself when you will have sex, you also must choose how far you will go. Your religious and moral beliefs, along with your goals, will help determine what feels right for you.

each other, so why allow myself to get so emotionally attached? We eventually stopped seeing each other. I realized that I was setting myself up for the same heartache I experienced when I had gone all the way.

The Varieties of Foreplay

Every form of affection outside intercourse can be considered foreplay. There are different levels of intensity, however. Holding hands, hugging, and light kissing are very mild forms of foreplay, whereas heavy petting and oral sex are more intense forms.

As you read through each form of foreplay, consider your feelings about each one. How do you want to deal with these issues in your own life?

Kissing.   Kissing can be very deceiving. Just as that little piece of pie looks totally harmless, we all know it's packed full of calories. I'm not saying we should never kiss, but we certainly need to consider how serious kissing really is. Once we begin kissing, a new precedent has been established and there's no turning back. In *Finding the Love of Your Life,* Dr. Neil Clark Warren writes, "Each level of sexual experience is so immediately rewarding that it's nearly impossible to be satisfied by previous levels."

One of the most important aspects of the dating process is getting to know the other person as deeply as possible and in as many different situations as possible. How can we effectively do this when we're obsessed with making out? As you read through chapter 13 on what qualities to look for in a man, you'll understand why it's smart to postpone being physical for as long as possible.

I can't tell you not to kiss until *x* amount of time has passed. That would be pointless. But I would like to caution you to take your time. Don't be afraid to say no until you are sure your feelings for each other are strong and real.

Holding Hands and Light Affection.   Holding hands and light affection are like vegetables. They're good for you—low in calories. Go ahead and have as much as you like, provided you don't add anything, like butter or some of the heavier forms of affection.

Cuddling.   Everybody loves to cuddle. And cuddling is fine as long as you're prepared to deal with the potential hazards. Very few people cuddle without kissing, and we all know kissing leads to other things.

I've also found that most women can cuddle for a lot longer than men without anything else ever happening. We just enjoy cuddling and being close. Men, however, usually see it as a prelude to something more.

Oral Sex and Petting.   Unless you want to have sex, don't engage in oral sex or petting. Couples who go this far typically end up going all the way.

Spending the Night Together.   I know some couples who have spent the night together but didn't do anything. I also know many couples who tried not to do anything but ended up going much further than they had intended. It's very risky. The final decision is up to you as to how far you are willing to go. But you may want to follow this rule: *If you don't want to have sex, or something equally as intimate, don't allow him in your bed!*

How to Say No to Kissing and Other Forms of Affection

When your date attempts to kiss you and you're not interested in participating, simply put your hand on his shoulder, pull away a little, and say, "Please don't take this personally, but I don't feel comfortable kissing this early in our relationship. I'd rather take it slow and just get to know you better." Or turn your head so that his kiss falls on your cheek, which is a great way to give him the message without being too blunt. Giving *him* a kiss on the cheek is also acceptable. He may frown, but he won't feel as slighted as if you push him away without any explanation or reassurance that it's not personal.

Giving him a short hug good-bye is also a warm way of saying good-night. If he's a nice guy, he will be polite and accept your feelings. He may even feel relieved not to be under pressure to sexually pursue you.

Some men may be hurt or slightly offended, but don't worry about that. If you're honest, sincere, and kind, any decent man will respect your wishes. If he gives you a hard time, then you may want to reconsider your interest in him.

If you don't feel comfortable with any form of affection early in the relationship, you could say, "Please don't be offended, but I'd rather not be affectionate until we know each other a little better. I really like you, but I move slowly when it comes to being physical. I don't want to get too distracted from getting to know you."

If he says something like, "I'm only wanting to hold your hand, for heaven's sake!" then just tell him you realize it's no big deal, but you just aren't comfortable with it right now. It's not that you're not a physical person, you just don't jump into these things so easily.

After you have been dating awhile, he may invite you over to watch a movie. If you feel brave and decide to go, you will need some strong comebacks for any potential advances. You are already armed with many responses from the previous chapter, but in terms of just foreplay, try these:

He may suggest that you lie on the floor with him or on the couch. Simply say, "If you don't mind, I'd rather sit over here. I just don't feel comfortable cuddling at this point in our friendship (or relationship)." If he persists or tries to convince you that it's harmless, just keep saying, "I'd really rather not, I'm just not comfortable with it." Eventually he'll give up. Remember, you can always leave. He needs to know that you mean what you say.

If you've made it as far as heavy petting, you probably should have said no a long time ago. But it's never too late to start over. You can say, "This has really gone too far. As much as I'm enjoying this, I know it isn't right. Not now anyway. I'd like to stop all of this, including kissing so much, and just develop other aspects of our relationship more." This is where your self-discipline has to take over because putting all physical contact on the back burner will be more difficult than ever.

I've had a lot of women tell me that sexual advances from men can sometimes be frightening. We rarely are taught how to deal with advances, so these situations can be scary, especially when we're young and inexperienced. I think we need to tell men how we feel. There's nothing wrong with saying, "You're making me feel very uncomfortable and frightened. Please don't do that, I'm just not ready." It's okay to admit we're afraid, and men need to know how their actions affect us.

As harmless as "making out" may seem, it can bring us tremendous frustration, pain, and unhappiness.

Wanda: I made myself crazy when I dated Kyle. I told him that premarital sex was out of the question, which he accepted. Part of the reason he accepted so easily was because he planned on doing everything except intercourse! He preferred going all the way, but heavy petting and oral sex was the next best thing.

I went along with this for awhile because I too have strong sexual desires, and I didn't want to lose him. I thought I had to do *something* to keep him interested. But every time we got into a heavy make-out session, I began to feel remorseful. Even though I was participating, I really didn't want that in my life! The fact that I was allowing it in my life brought me a lot of unhappiness. And frankly, by engaging in foreplay, our relationship wasn't at all strengthened.

◇◇◇

Beatrice: As I look back on my relationship with Todd, I'm amazed I was even able to focus on anything other than our relationship. I was consumed with fear and self-doubt because, on one hand, I absolutely did not want to engage in heavy foreplay but, on the other hand, I really wanted to be with him. We were obsessed with each other sexually. We had already gone all the way once, but we made a promise to stop. But we couldn't stop making out, nor did we really want to. If only we could have just kissed and held each other, without going any further! Maybe if it hadn't been so good between us, I would have had more resolve. But I just didn't have the power.

Masturbation

Your religious and moral convictions about masturbation will be the strongest determining factor as to whether you should engage in this practice. Are you able to engage in this practice without any negative feelings whatsoever?

Many people feel that masturbation is like drinking a sugar drink. It never really quenches your thirst. It might distract your thirst or "take the edge off," but the overall result is usually unsatisfying.

Masturbation can also sexually desensitize you. This can cause problems down the road with achieving orgasm because you have become so accustomed to getting there on your own.

Beatrice said it all when she said she lacked the power. That really is the heart of the matter, isn't it? If we all had the power, there wouldn't be a problem. But we aren't always able to call upon our will power to carry us through. This is where we can turn to God. We should call upon God to give us the added strength we lack.

The Three C's: Commitment, Confidence, and Consistency

If you are serious about putting sex and foreplay on the back burner until a deeper love has developed, then you will want to incorporate the Three C's into your life.

The commitment of abstinence is not just about abstaining from sexual activity. It's a commitment to care for your *body* and to treat it lovingly. It's a commitment to your *mind,* to keep it clear and healthy. When you are truly committed to abstinence there is absolutely no room for negotiation.

Obviously, to maintain this kind of commitment, you have to have confidence in yourself and your decision. You need to have a firm belief that what you are doing is absolutely right. You will gain this confidence as you become clearer about your reasons for abstaining and as you become more intent on achieving your goals.

Ralph Waldo Emerson wrote, "That which we persist in doing becomes easier for us to do; not that the nature of the thing itself is changed, but that our power to do so is increased." In other words, the more consistent we are, the easier it will get.

There will always be times when we will feel like tearing our hair out because of our desire to be sexual. We literally have to train ourselves to just feel the feelings and then redirect our energies elsewhere. You can do it!

12

The Ten Qualities Men Find Most *Irresistible* in a Lifetime Mate

We all want to be attractive to men. But to be *irresistible* would be fantastic! There are many traits that men are *initially* attracted to, but we need to know what it is they look for in a *wife*. Some women seem to have some magical quality that draws men to them like a magnet. They never lack for dates, and everywhere they go, men take notice. But many of these women aren't necessarily beautiful in a physical sense. They might be physically beautiful, but that certainly wouldn't be enough to hold a man's attention for long.

Men have to *want* to ask us out, so we do what we can to increase the odds that they will do so. This doesn't mean that we change our entire personalities or become something we're not just for the sake of getting their attention. There will always be someone out there who will appreciate us for who we are.

But there are certain qualities that men find particularly appealing—and even irresistible—in a woman.

These qualities not only draw men to us, they bring *us* greater happiness. Just as we appreciate men who are confident, intelligent, and hard-working, men appreciate certain strengths in women.

Men may appreciate other qualities than the ones I mention, such as athletic ability, wit, great cooking skills, or intelligence. But the qualities mentioned in this chapter are what make a woman a great wife, partner, and friend.

Men are the natural pursuers. We need to listen to what *they* find attractive in a woman. Many women today have this attitude: "This is who I am. Take me or leave me! If you don't like what you see . . . tough!" They lack mysteriousness and feminine charm. They may blurt out all of their flaws and air their dirty laundry, landing bombshell after bombshell on the men they meet. Then, they wonder why he doesn't continue to call.

If we strive to develop the qualities mentioned in this chapter, men will continue to pursue us.

Appearance Is Not the Most Important Thing

Contrary to what most people think, a woman's appearance is not the most important issue for a man. Men want a woman who is clean, healthy, radiant, and takes care of herself, but she doesn't have to be drop-dead gorgeous. The fact is, men become more attracted to a woman as they fall in love with her, until eventually they do think she's gorgeous! That's the wonderful part about love. Just as having sex with a man causes us to bond emotionally and see him in a different light, love has the same effect on a man. The feeling of love he has for the woman transforms her in his eyes. If she happened to be physically beautiful before, she is even more beautiful now.

If we look around us, we can see that men do fall in love with and marry women who are not necessarily beautiful. There are women who are overweight, who have serious skin problems, who have irregular features, or even serious handicaps who have men in their lives who absolutely adore them. On the flip side, we also see absolutely gorgeous women who can't keep a man.

A woman's appearance initially may be what draws a man to her, but not always. It can be the sparkle in her eyes or her bright smile. Maybe she has a great personality that radiates from her. In fact, women who aren't all that physically attractive often win the best

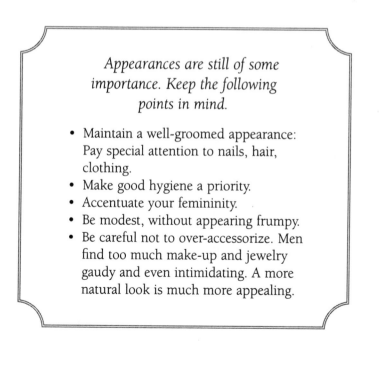

Appearances are still of some importance. Keep the following points in mind.

- Maintain a well-groomed appearance: Pay special attention to nails, hair, clothing.
- Make good hygiene a priority.
- Accentuate your femininity.
- Be modest, without appearing frumpy.
- Be careful not to over-accessorize. Men find too much make-up and jewelry gaudy and even intimidating. A more natural look is much more appealing.

men because they work harder at developing irresistible attributes.

The Ten Qualities

Through research, my own personal experience, and simply observing those around me, I came up with the following ten qualities. After a brief description of each quality are a few questions to ask yourself. These questions are designed to get you thinking about the issues.

Get out a notebook and write your answers to these questions and spend some time considering them. You are guaranteed to gain greater insight. Following the questions, I list suggestions to follow for one week. You can come up with your own additional ways to make improvements. By incorporating the suggestions into your daily routine, they can become a part of you.

1. Femininity

Many women today have abandoned their femininity and instead have brought to the forefront their more masculine side. This might have seemed necessary to succeed in business, but as they've gained respect, these women haven't always gained love. Now many women are attempting to get back in touch with their femininity. They want to develop their softer, more gentle side. Developing her femininity makes a woman more appealing to men, and it brings her greater fulfillment and joy.

In her book *Being a Woman,* Dr. Toni Grant describes the ideal woman by describing the "Madonna" and "courtesan" aspects of the feminine personality. The Madonna is the spiritual and inspirational side; the courtesan is the playful, sensual side. Grant writes, "The woman who embraces both the Madonna and Courtesan aspects of feminine personality is irresistible to men. Her Madonna is idealistic and unattainable; her Courtesan is visceral and enticing. Utilizing these two powerful aspects of femininity, women civilize and domesticate men, channel their sexual energies, and inspire them to greatness."

What Is Femininity?

Femininity is more than just being female. It is a *way of being*. It is a certain softness, gentleness, and tenderness within a woman's nature. This quality can be seen in her appearance, movements, voice, and manner.

Femininity is the opposite of masculinity, which is typically more aggressive, harsh, tough, and loud. Being a truly feminine woman will attract more men to you than anything else. *Men are magnetized by feminine women.* They are fascinated, intrigued, inspired, and amused by the feminine creature who is so clearly different than they are. The feminine quality instantly awakens the chivalrous, manly qualities in him. When a man is in the presence of a woman who is not in touch with her feminine side, he sees her as just a person and will treat her accordingly. He will most likely be cordial and friendly, but his instincts of wanting to protect, cherish, and adore won't be awakened. A good example of this is a woman who acts as though she is "one of the guys." If you want to be noticed in a romantic sense, you'll definitely want to be seen as feminine.

How to Bring Out Your Feminine Side

In bringing out your feminine side, the key lies in the way you look, feel, smell, talk, walk, and act. Take a look at women who seem to epitomize this. They are all around us, even though they may be less common. They seem to love being women. They wear feminine clothing such as dresses, skirts, flowered prints, hats. They wear perfume and sometimes wear barrettes and bows in their hair. They speak in a soft voice; they aren't loud, boisterous, or obnoxious. They have a gracious, calm spirit about them.

The following are definitions of some of the qualities that make up a truly feminine woman.

Gracious: Marked by kindness and courtesy. Marked by tact and delicacy. Merciful, compassionate. Characterized by elegance and good taste.

Dignified: Esteemed or honored. Showing poise and self-respect.

Serene: Unruffled, tranquil. Unclouded.

Peaceful: Undisturbed by strife, turmoil, or disagreement. Tranquil. Opposed to strife.

Ask Yourself:

How feminine am I in my appearance, manner, movements, and overall energy?

Do I love being a woman and does it show?

Do men comment on how feminine I am?

Try This:

For one week I will:

- Wear the most feminine clothes I have, or I will purchase a particularly feminine outfit. I will pay close attention to how this makes me feel and how men respond to me.

- Allow my softer, more tender side to come out.

- Observe highly feminine women and see what they do differently than women who are less feminine. I will observe the difference in how men respond to them.

2. Strength of Character

A person's "character" refers to their combined moral or ethical structure. Some of the qualities that strengthen character are honesty, integrity, loyalty, patience, tolerance, humility, trustworthiness, and unselfishness.

Unselfishness is key to a strong character. None of us is above serving others, and we should help those who are less fortunate. We can volunteer to clean someone's home or take food to the sick or needy.

A woman with strong character *doesn't allow others to abuse her or mistreat her in any way.* A woman lacks inner strength if she allows a man to walk all over her and doesn't command respect. This includes being lied to, deceived, treated in a cold and unloving manner, being dominated and controlled, and constantly being criticized or belittled. How we handle this kind of treatment is indicative of the level of inner strength we have.

Mary was tired of Tim making promises and then never keeping them. If he said he'd pick her up at seven, he would show up at eight. Sometimes he wouldn't show up at all and then make a lame excuse. He made a habit out of taking advantage of Mary and had little regard for her feelings. But the way Mary chose to deal with the problem was to complain and argue with Tim. Whenever Tim showed up late, she would yell at him and they would get into a huge fight. She would try to explain her feelings and tell him how much it hurt her when he treated her this way, but nothing worked. His behavior would improve for a short time, but eventually he'd revert back to his old ways.

Mary was allowing Tim to mistreat her because she continued to remain in the situation. Many women make the mistake of thinking that if they are complaining or fighting for their rights, they are being strong and not allowing the mistreatment. All they are really doing, though, is creating more aggravation for themselves and their mate. Whining, complaining, and threatening mean nothing when it comes to mistreatment. Initially Mary needed to voice her feelings, but after the second time, she needed to make a decision: Either stay and accept the treatment, or leave. To remain in the relationship and endure any form of abuse is the same as accepting it, even though you may complain vehemently.

Note: I am only referring here to serious mistreatment or abuse. There are times when men become preoccupied with work or may seem uncaring due to other reasons, but this doesn't necessarily constitute mistreatment.

Ask Yourself:

What is my character like? Create a checklist to include honesty, integrity, patience, unselfishness, loyalty, humility, and tolerance.

What would others say about my character?

Which areas need the most work, and what can I do to improve?

Do I allow men to mistreat me in any way?

Try This:

For one week I will:

- Make a concerted effort to be honest in every way. I will choose a different quality to work on each week.

- Not speak negatively about anyone. I will not criticize others.

- Pray for a change in my character.

- Conduct a spring-cleaning on myself. I will make a checklist of all the areas in my life and determine which areas need work—character, spiritual needs, work goals, amends to be made, and fears to be conquered.

- Find some way to be of service. I will make this a regular part of my life.

3. Vulnerability

I have asked many men what one quality in a woman has the greatest impact on them. Remarkably, I get the same answer from all: vulnerability. There is something appealing about this quality for a man. It brings out their protective side. He feels she *needs* him. It also makes him feel invincible. On the other hand, men don't want a *needy* woman. There is an art to balancing vulnerability with strength, but once mastered, you will definitely stand out as special and unique in men's eyes.

One day a male friend and I were analyzing various famous women, and he was telling me how he felt about each one. This is an excellent exercise, by the way, to do with your male friends in order to find out what men really think. I like to ask the question, "What feeling does that woman awaken in you?" You'd be surprised at how candid the answers are. Some men just aren't going to have a clear answer, but if he's the type to engage in this sort of exercise, you can learn a lot.

Men were crazy for Marilyn Monroe, and the majority of them said her vulnerability was her most appealing quality. Men felt an overwhelming desire to take care of her and protect her when in her presence. She obviously had problems in other areas of her life, but we can't ignore the incredible attraction that men all over the world had for her.

Some women today see being vulnerable as a serious weakness, and maybe it is in the business world. But when it comes to love, the rules change. The opposite of being vulnerable is to be in total control without needing anyone else. Men may *respect* that in a person, but they won't necessarily be attracted to it in the romantic sense. They may even get turned off.

I once watched a couple shopping in the mall. The woman was carrying a very large bag filled with merchandise from one of the department stores. Her boyfriend was trying to get her to give him the bag to carry, because it was so heavy. She vehemently refused. Although they were wrestling with it in a playful sort of way, this woman made it very clear that she didn't need his help—she could do just fine on her own. Maybe she could in that particular instance, but she missed out on a wonderful opportunity to let him come to her aid. This may seem like a silly, insignificant situation, but it's these small, brief moments that make men feel needed and that enhance a relationship.

Contrary to popular belief, we do need men. We don't need them to validate us as worthy human beings or to be responsible for our happiness, but we do need them. They offer physical protection. Many men have excellent problem-solving skills. I know that I have the ability to come up with solutions, but I know that men have a different perspective, and I like to hear it. More important, we need a man with whom to create a family. Very few of us wish to grow old alone, without someone to love who will also love us.

By admitting that we need men, we are not claiming that we are weak, incapable creatures. We are conceding that we are in touch with the reality that men and women are different in many respects, and we acknowledge and appreciate those differences. We are confident enough in ourselves and in our femininity that we are able to turn to men for their strengths.

Some men may take advantage of this and try to control and dominate us, or they'll see us as being less than adequate. They may even be somewhat abusive. This is not healthy. When an abusive situation begins, we need to quickly set a new standard. We need to immediately let him know that we will not stand for any kind of mistreatment and that we are not interested in being controlled by anyone. This will usually correct the problem, but if not, we need to reconsider our involvement.

Ask Yourself:

Do I appear to need a man or do I seem too controlling?

Am I afraid of being vulnerable—possibly because of a negative experience?

What are some of the ways I can let down my guard and begin to show that I am not invincible?

Try This:

For one week I will:

- Ask men for help, whether it be for advice, guidance, or moral support. I will show them that I need them.

- Let my fears show. If I feel the need to cry, I will do so without being ashamed. I won't come across as all-knowing or all-powerful.

- I will let my guard down by showing my weaknesses at times. I'll notice the difference in how men react and in how I'll feel.

4. Lovingness

Men need to know that the woman they marry has a nurturing, caring nature.

Barry described how much he appreciated this trait in his wife.

When my wife and I were first dating, I had the opportunity of seeing her interact with her nieces and nephews. I've always been mesmerized by how loving and kind she is with them. They just love her, and I could see why. She never loses her patience, she just knows how to make them feel special. In fact, she's that way with everyone, which is partly why I fell in love with her. How could I resist someone so good?

Becoming a more loving woman requires finding ways to show people that we care. It means listening patiently when others are in need of an understanding friend. It means giving our time and attention. We become more loving as we let go of resentments and learn to forgive. As we let go of old anger, worry, and fear, our hearts and souls expand and we are better able to give and receive love. Equally important, as our self-esteem improves, so does our capacity to love.

Ask Yourself:

Am I a loving and caring person?

In what ways am I loving? How do I show I care?

What are some ways I can work at being more loving?

Do I still have unresolved anger and resentments?

What else might be holding me back from being a nurturing, unselfish, loving person?

Try This:

For one week I will:

- Not criticize my boyfriend. I will only encourage and appreciate him.
- Do something nice for my parents, such as cook dinner or run errands for them.

- Be more patient with the person at work who drives me crazy. I will find ways to actually help them with their duties.

- Ask those I come into contact with how they are. I will truly listen and show them that I care, either by being sympathetic and understanding or finding ways to assist them.

- Tell my closest friends and family members that I love and appreciate them.

5. Happiness

Having happiness doesn't mean everything always goes perfectly. It does mean that we are able to be calm and content in the face of adversity and that we are grateful for what we have.

Men appreciate a woman who is happy and has a sense of gratitude for what she has. This makes sense when we consider the opposite, which would be a woman who is depressed, moody, and melancholy. Men feel responsible when we're unhappy—they think *they* aren't able to make us happy. It gives men great pleasure to see us full of joy. If a man feels he can't make you happy, he's not going to be eager to make a life-long commitment.

Regardless of how hard men try to make us happy, *we* are ultimately responsible for our own happiness. We need to create peace of mind and contentedness for ourselves, whether we're alone, in a relationship, or married.

Ask Yourself:

Am I basically a happy person?

What is my level of joy?

What could be holding me back from being happy?

Do I want to achieve a greater level of happiness?

Try This:

For one week I will:

- Act as if I am already a happy person. I will smile at everyone I pass by and exude enthusiasm and energy.
- Not complain about my problems.
- Make a list of things for which I am grateful.
- Thank God for all I have.

6. Healthfulness

Men are drawn to healthy women. But true, enduring health is more than just being free from illness. When we are healthy, we sparkle. Our eyes are bright and clear. We are more radiant and appear to be more cheerful. Our skin has a healthy glow and we look rested.

When we are healthy emotionally and spiritually, as well as physically, the effect is stunning. I realize this balance isn't easy to maintain; our hormones and monthly cycles seriously affect our attitudes and moods. But if we make it a priority to maintain a healthy glow, we will experience a difference.

On the most basic level we can improve our health and overall moods by drinking lots of water, getting seven to eight hours sleep every night, eating nutritious foods, and eliminating harmful substances such as tobacco, alcohol, and caffeine. Including some sort of physical exercise in your daily routine is also very important.

Ask Yourself:

Do I possess a healthy glow? Has anyone ever commented on how radiant or healthy I appear?

Do I have a lot of energy and vitality?

Do I complain about my health often?

What could be sapping my energy or negatively affecting my health?

What can I do to improve my health?

Try This:

For one week I will:

- Eliminate excess fat from my diet.
- Drink two quarts of water a day.
- Begin taking walks or going to the gym.
- Make sure that my hair and skin are clean, shiny, and healthy looking.

7. Responsibility

Responsibility means following through with promises, being on time, and doing what needs to be done on a daily basis, especially those things we say we are going to do.

I used to know a woman who was always in debt, who was afraid of answering the phone because it might be a creditor. Unopened bills were lying around her apartment for months. She didn't even look at them! Yet she wouldn't think twice about going out and buying a whole new outfit. Would we think of behaving this way if we had children? In preparing for marriage and motherhood, this is one of the first areas we need to work on.

Being responsible means being organized. We need to create a simple budget for ourselves, set up a filing system, keep track of appointments, and set goals. We want to be responsible for our own welfare, but we also need to recognize the tremendous importance men place on this quality.

Mark has had his fair share of flaky women.

> I don't know what it is, but I keep attracting women who can't seem to get it together. My last girlfriend was constantly late. Her car was always out of gas and breaking down, because she didn't handle the maintenance. If I asked her to do me a favor, she invariably forgot. I just couldn't count on her. It made me crazy! I couldn't imagine being married to her. She'd probably forget to feed the kids!

A responsible woman is *able to deal with problems.* Life is full of tragedies and sudden changes that can often throw us off kilter emotionally. While a man appreciates a woman who needs him and his masculine protection, he also wants her to show strength and courage when a crisis occurs. He likes to know that she can rise to the occasion, rather than fall apart.

Being self-disciplined is yet another part of being responsible. None of us is perfectly self-disciplined. We procrastinate and avoid doing certain things such as exercising, dieting, or quitting smoking. It's very hard to be disciplined, but it's worth it.

Being able not to have sex until it's right is a good sign that you are a disciplined woman. Men take these things into account, even though they may never voice their thoughts. It's also important to be disciplined in showing up for work, paying our bills, staying in shape, avoiding overindulging, and maintaining spiritual balance.

Ask Yourself:

Am I a responsible person? Am I on time, do I follow through, am I reliable?

Do I have self-control? Am I independent or needy?

In what ways can I improve?

Try This:

For one week I will:

- Make a point to be on time no matter what.
- Fulfill my promises and follow through with commitments.
- Return all calls within one day.
- Get completely organized. I will see the difference in how I feel and in how others react to me.
- Practice being more self-disciplined.

8. Flexibility

Men especially appreciate a woman who can be flexible. It's not so much that men mind us having strong opinions about various issues, it's when we absolutely *oppose* their way of thinking or their plans. My ex-boyfriend used to say I was "digging in my heels," and being "too tough." And I was. I must admit, it didn't get me very far. It only alienated my partner and made me feel horrible.

One day as I was jogging, I saw a couple standing alongside a car, arguing over who was going to drive. He said he wanted to drive, but she insisted *she* would do the driving. If that woman understood that sometimes men need to feel that they are in charge—which doesn't take away from her, but only brings more harmony into the relationship—I'm sure she would have gladly let him drive. It would have been a small sacrifice with great rewards. Especially in today's world, we need to look for small opportunities like these, where we can allow a man to feel like our hero, our knight in shining armor.

Sometimes we think we have to be right at all costs, but typically that cost is just too high. Part of being flexible is having a good attitude. I am not suggesting that you suppress any negative feelings you may have or pretend to be pleasant when you feel like the dragon lady. I merely suggest you take a look at your general attitude. A good attitude means that even though things may not be going the way we would like them to, we can still have a positive outlook. We don't "lose it," become irritated, or get a sour look on our faces every time something goes wrong.

We should be able to look at a situation and ask ourselves, "How important is it, really?"

Ask Yourself:

Am I too stubborn in my relationships with men? Do I always have to be right?

How flexible am I in general?

What would others say about my level of flexibility?

What could be causing my lack of flexibility?

Are my priorities in order?

Try This:

For one week I will:

- Not argue with my mate or anyone else.

- Make a special effort to see the other person's side of the situation and strive to be more understanding.

- Ask my partner (if you are in a relationship) to further explain his position instead of arguing so that I can gain more insight into his views.

- Not fight my partner in every situation. I will practice doing things his way unless they go against my morals or values. I will observe the difference in how he responds and how much our relationship improves.

9. Inner Peacefulness

One man I interviewed said, "I'm attracted to a woman who has a calm demeanor and lacks all outward signs of neurosis." Having inner peace means having a calm spirit even though there may be chaos all around us. It means not being easily rattled. If we don't have inner peace, we can come across as neurotic. A woman without inner peace worries over the smallest things. She can't seem to handle any small tragedy or occurrence.

Having a strong sense of inner peace is not beyond our reach. Anyone can acquire it, but like anything else of great value, it takes effort. It is impossible to have inner peace if we are harboring resentments, anger, or are not dealing with our fears. If we have a lot of skeletons in our closet, we will need to face them. Making amends and cleaning up our life in every area paves the way for peace. Also, knowing who we are and what we stand for gives us peace and confidence.

Ask Yourself:

Do I possess a calm, peaceful spirit? If not, what might be the cause?

Do I constantly worry about things that are out of my control?

Am I able to sit still and do nothing without going crazy?

Am I petrified of people and life in general?

What can I do to develop a peaceful spirit?

Try This:

For one week I will:

- Pray for peace of mind and serenity.
- Practice sitting still and being calm.
- Read something spiritual.
- Seek those who have peace to observe them and ask for guidance.

10. Playfulness

Men go crazy for playfulness. Why? Because playfulness represents everything that is delightful. This quality charms men and takes away some of their seriousness. It is a wonderful way to lighten his mood and bring out *his* more playful side.

Part of having a playful attitude is having spunk. If we only develop the sweeter, kinder side of ourselves without having some fire or backbone, we will appear to be too docile or submissive. Justin shared this with me:

> I need a woman who won't let me take advantage of her. It isn't that I want to take advantage, but if I know I can get away with it, I don't treat her as well. I guess it's human nature. I like a woman who will put me in my place if that's what I need.

Another perspective comes from Joey:

> A woman who is a bit feisty is very intriguing. If she's just too nice or easy-going, I find her a little on the boring side. But a woman with spunk is exciting. She can take it too far of course, but just the right amount is very attractive.

Spunk comes from having confidence and not being easily controlled. When we have this quality, we feel free to say what's on our minds without apology or explanation. We aren't constantly trying to people-please or acquiesce.

Playfulness and spunk are childlike qualities. Not only are they appealing to men, but they are excellent ways to express ourselves to men without alienating them. In describing these qualities in little girls, Helen Andelin, author of *Fascinating Womanhood* writes,

> They are so trusting, so sincere, and so innocent, and yet so piquant and outspoken that they are often teased into anger. They are too innocent to feel hate, jealousy, resentment, and the uglier emotions. When such a child is teased, she does not respond with some hideous sarcasm. Instead, she stamps her foot

and shakes her curls and pouts. She gets adorably angry at herself because her efforts to respond are impotent.

How do others, especially men, respond to this type of behavior? Mrs. Andelin writes,

> We feel an irresistible longing to pick up such a child and hug it. We would do anything rather than permit such an adorable little thing to suffer danger or want; to protect and care for such a delightfully human little creature would be nothing less than a delight. This is much the same feeling that a woman inspires in a man when she expresses anger in a childlike way. Her ridiculous exaggeration of manner makes him suddenly want to laugh; makes him feel, in contrast, stronger, more sensible and more of a man. This is why women who are little spitfires—independent and saucy—are often sought after by men. This anger, however, must be the sauciness of a child, and not the intractable stubbornness of a woman well able to "kill her own snakes."

We need to develop and use our childlike side, not as a way to manipulate or change a man, but rather to give us a way to express our feelings. This is much better than suppressing them. We also know from experience that expressing intense feelings of anger, resentment, bitterness, and rage, never works—it only destroys love. Childlike qualities bring out feelings of love and tenderness in a man and brings a couple closer together.

Ask Yourself:

Do I have a playful, teasing spirit, or am I too serious and uptight?

Am I a people-pleaser, or do I do what is right for me?

Do I have backbone and not allow others to walk all over me?

Am I so feisty that I'm obnoxious or too tough?

Try This:

For one week I will:

- Practice being playful and flirtatious. I will watch little girls and observe how they act, since this quality comes so naturally to them.

- Practice being spunky even though it may seem unnatural or awkward. I will pay close attention to how men respond.

- Notice other women who seem to possess this quality and observe how they act and the responses they receive.

- Not allow anyone to walk all over me or abuse me in any way. I will stand up for myself and voice my opinions and feelings.

- Be more open with my emotions in a playful, childlike way.

- Find ways to make my life more interesting and full.

❖ ❖ ❖

If you are feeling a little overwhelmed with all the work you have to do on yourself, take comfort in the fact that you already possess many of these qualities right now. Sometimes we're so hard on ourselves that

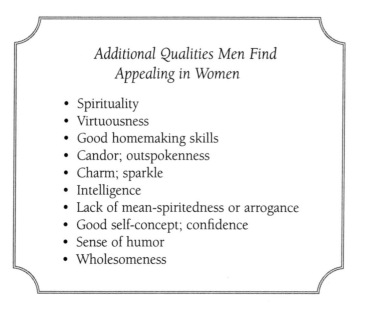

*Additional Qualities Men Find
Appealing in Women*

- Spirituality
- Virtuousness
- Good homemaking skills
- Candor; outspokenness
- Charm; sparkle
- Intelligence
- Lack of mean-spiritedness or arrogance
- Good self-concept; confidence
- Sense of humor
- Wholesomeness

we don't give ourselves credit for what we do right. Perhaps making a list of your positive qualities will help remind you. As they say in twelve-step programs, we are striving for *progress, not perfection.*

13

What You Need to Know About Him Before Being Physical

One of the most important things we can do for ourselves is to take our time to really get to know the men we date before being physical on any level. Because we emotionally bond so strongly through foreplay and sex, it's imperative that we do. Otherwise, we end up thinking we're in love with someone with whom we're really not compatible. The longer we put off physical contact and get to know as much about him as possible, the better.

What you need to know prior to being intimate is very simple: It's the same information you need to know to determine if he is someone you see yourself having a long-term relationship with. In other words, is he someone you want to spend the rest of your life with? You don't have to know all the information I list in this chapter before getting into a relationship; these are things you will learn *as you date*. It doesn't take long to learn some of the most pertinent information about a person. In fact, often times it's within the first few minutes of meeting a man that we learn much of what we need to know. Our first instincts are amazingly accurate. The problem is, we usually ignore them.

Look at the Facts

Sometimes we don't want to know the truth about a man because we want to be in a relationship so badly. If you find yourself spending weeks, months, or even years with men who are wrong for you, then this chapter is for you. It is not designed to keep you out of dead-end relationships, but it can help you know what to look for, and what to pay special attention to.

I doubt you will ever find a man who possesses all of the following qualities. He would be just a little too perfect. And you would remain single for a very long time if you were looking for a man with all of these traits. Use the information in this chapter as a guide to help you determine which qualities you want and need in a mate and which ones you can live without.

Create Your "Man Plan"

As you study this chapter and determine what is essential for you in a mate, you will want to create what I call a "Man Plan." This will be your road map, which lists those qualities you want in a man. This is not etched in stone, however. Your tastes and desires will change over time, and you will need to be flexible. Also, you don't want to make it impossible for yourself to meet someone. So be careful that you do not make the list so long and picky that no one could fit the bill.

Take out your notebook or journal and write, "Man Plan" at the top of a page. Then, go through this chapter, and write down the areas and qualities I have outlined. Add any qualities that are important to you that I may not have mentioned.

Qualities to Look for

We all have different tastes and desires. There are a million different personality types out there. You may like a real aggressive, go-getter type who is highly intelligent and witty. Or you may prefer a more reserved, shy type. What turns one woman on may completely appall another.

No Addictions

It's obvious that we don't want to end up with an alcoholic and/or drug addict, and yet many women do. Be extra cautious and observant in this area, because life with an addict is no fun. He doesn't have to be a skid-row, morning drinker to be an alcoholic. He could be what is called a *period drinker,* which means he only gets drunk periodically, but he still has a problem. It isn't how much he drinks that matters, it's what happens to him when he does drink. Is he consistently able to have one or two and then just stop? Or does he seem to lose control once he starts? He may hold a good job and appear to have it all together, and yet still be a "functioning alcoholic." If you have a slight hunch that he may have a problem, then you are probably right.

If you are seeing someone who you think might have a problem, you could suggest that they get help (I recommend Alcoholics Anonymous). But I've learned that you can't help an alcoholic unless he is willing to help himself. If he isn't ready to admit he has a problem, and he isn't at a point where he is willing to do whatever it takes to quit, then he just isn't ready, and there is nothing you can do. The worst thing you could do is enable him to continue drinking by taking care of him. Sometimes the best thing we can do for someone with a problem is to let them go so that they can hit bottom and eventually get the help they need.

A Strong Character

In choosing a mate, the most important area to consider is his character. He may be handsome, intelligent, fun, and successful—but if he lacks important character qualities such as integrity, unselfishness, self-discipline, honesty, loyalty, humility, dignity, and dependability, then you have an empty shell of a man.

Notice how unselfish he is. Is he self-absorbed? Does he sacrifice his time, money, and feelings in order to add to the well-being of his friends and family? Pay particular attention to how honest he is in his dealings with you and with others. Do you often feel that he isn't being straight with you or that you can't figure out where he's coming from? Being married to a dishonest man means a lifetime of frustration and unhappiness.

Consider his level of self-worth. Is he a man with dignity? If he feels that he is worthy of honor and respect, he won't allow others to belittle or abuse him. He commands a certain amount of respect. Equally important to confidence and dignity is humility. Living with an arrogant man who is unwilling to admit his faults can be a nightmare.

Can you count on this man? A life of uncertainty and frustration is likely to result if you marry a man who isn't dependable. A loyal, faithful man is the only type of man to marry. There is no guarantee that he will always be there for you and remain faithful, but be very cautious and take your time in getting to know him well before making a permanent commitment.

Confidence

I met a man recently who was very handsome, well-dressed, and intelligent-looking. We happened to bump into each other, and we said hello. I asked him a question. I was very surprised to see that he couldn't look me in the eyes. He spoke so quietly, almost under his breath. I had to ask him to speak up. He came across as timid and unsure of himself. He lacked confidence. I was shocked to see this entirely different man emerge than the one I saw before me. I must admit I was disappointed. I'm sure he's a great guy with many wonderful qualities, but when a man lacks confidence, it changes the entire impression, and women usually find it very unattractive.

You probably already know that you are attracted to confident men. But confidence in a man is important for lots of reasons, not only because it's so attractive to us. A confident man believes in his own capabilities, feels that he is competent, and does not feel inadequate. He realizes he's not invincible and that he has limitations, but he carries himself in such a way that instills trust.

The main reason you may want to find a confident man is so that you will be able to trust in his judgment and believe in him. We *respect* men who are confident, even if they don't always do the right thing.

Masculinity

Nothing is more appealing than a masculine man. Commercials show shirtless men with muscles bursting and sweat dripping off them while they guzzle down soda. Movies depict men who are invincible and always get the beautiful woman. Just as men are attracted to very feminine women, women are attracted to very masculine men.

Masculinity is so appealing because it brings out our femininity. And this is what creates "chemistry." This is why we want to *enhance* the differences between the sexes, rather than become more similar. Look for a man who naturally makes you feel like a woman, and who awakens romantic feelings within you.

The following list of qualities are typically considered masculine.

- Independence
- Aggressiveness
- Fearlessness
- Capability
- Decisiveness

Leadership

Even if you are striving for equality in a relationship, you will want to look for a man with leadership qualities, especially if you plan to stay home while raising your children.

A leader commands respect and instills trust. If you don't feel this way about your man, there could be serious problems down the road. A woman who doesn't respect her husband eventually has contempt for him. A married friend of mine once said, "I'm nothing more than a guest in my own house. I'm only there to take orders and serve my wife's needs." His wife obviously had some problems, but he also had failed to win his wife's respect.

A man who is a real leader takes control of his life and doesn't rely on others to run it for him. (He doesn't, however, constantly try to control you.) He knows how to make decisions and stick to them. He is strong, yet fair. Some of his strongest traits are the following:

He doesn't compromise.   He doesn't go against what he knows to be right. He follows his conscience. He may take other's opinions into consideration, but he makes up his own mind and doesn't compromise, especially when it comes to ethical and moral issues.

He doesn't shirk responsibilities.   A leader realizes his responsibilities and fulfills them. He doesn't try to get out of them. This doesn't mean that he never struggles with responsibilities, but he doesn't hide and try to push them onto others. In most cases, he thrives on assuming responsibility. Although it can be scary for him to have overwhelming responsibilities, such as a family, he loves the feeling it gives him. He loves providing for his family and making them happy.

He doesn't allow others to dominate him.   He is his own man. No one can walk all over him or tell him what to do. This is not to say that he's stubborn; he is just independent and feels he is capable of solving his own problems and making his own decisions.

He has humility.   As strong a leader as he might be, if he doesn't have humility, he will come across as arrogant, mean, and unfair. Humility is a very attractive quality in a man, especially the more capable and gifted he is. A humble man knows his strengths, yet also realizes his limitations. He knows he isn't perfect or invincible. He knows he needs to consult others in many situations. He knows he doesn't "own" people and that they have rights also.

He has a desire to protect women and children. With the confusion of roles today, men aren't sure if women want chivalry. But many women prefer a man who has the desire to protect. It doesn't mean you aren't equal in value or intelligence. It is a matter of appreciating the differences. It's wonderful to see a man who is concerned about the welfare of women and children, and nothing is more revolting than a man who has the attitude that they should fend for themselves. Someone told me about several couples in Los Angeles who broke up during the earthquakes because many of the women didn't like the way the men responded. Some men were just too concerned with themselves. On the other hand, I saw on the news a couple who were married after the earthquake because of one man's chivalry. He saved the woman's life, and they fell in love. If you like this quality in a man, do what you can to awaken it in him. Let him know how much you appreciate his efforts.

He is able to overcome emotions.   A leader is able to overcome his emotions *when necessary*. He doesn't allow them to rule him or destroy his confidence. This is especially necessary in the face of an emergency. I am not saying that men shouldn't express their emotions. There is nothing wrong with men crying or expressing their feelings, but a certain amount of control over their emotions is preferable.

He is hard-working.   A leader is not lazy. He doesn't sleep all day, waiting for the unemployment check to arrive and then head over to Mom's just in time for dinner. He works hard, maybe even at two or three jobs in order to support his family. If he comes into hardship, he doesn't make excuses for his situation or blame it on others. He picks himself up and does what he can to fix the situation. He doesn't allow himself to be a charity case and does not want others to pity him.

He has a sense of humor.   A good leader is not overly serious. He is able to laugh at life and at himself. He knows how to "lighten up" and have a good time.

He is not overly insecure.   Some men are extremely insecure, and as a result, they can come across as very "needy." A true leader does not have this problem. If he has a bout of insecurity, he quickly overcomes it. Sometimes men who seem to have oversized egos are actually insecure underneath. They have to be "big shots" and are constantly trying to impress others because of their insecurities. A good leader knows he has flaws and weaknesses, yet he believes in himself.

A Good Provider

Even if you are financially secure and intend to stay that way, you may want a man who is also financially secure and who sees himself as the primary provider. Most women plan to stay home at least for awhile when they have children, and therefore they need someone who will assume the full responsibility of providing for the family.

He must be capable of providing the necessities of life: a roof over your head, food, medical attention when necessary, and so on. No matter what hardships may come his way, he feels responsible for being the primary provider for the family.

It's up to you to determine what level of financial security you need in order to be happy. We all come from various social classes. We all have different desires. One woman may be perfectly happy living in a small apartment with very few luxuries. Another woman may require more. There is nothing wrong with either one of these scenarios, it's really a matter of tastes and desires.

It is within a man's nature to want to provide for his family. This brings him tremendous joy and fulfillment. It makes him feel more manly and gives his life more meaning. He develops a healthy sense of pride and accomplishment as he takes on the huge responsibility of providing for his family.

Never look at a man simply as a paycheck, however, or as someone who is there to provide you with every little material wish. That is not his job in life. If he wants to shower you with gifts or other luxuries, that's up to him, but to *expect* it is impolite, unattractive, and even vulgar. Also, never take him for granted. He works hard to provide you with the best life has to offer, and he needs to be appreciated for that.

The following are a few points of concern in the area of finances.

Is he responsible with money?   Watch out for men who aren't good with money. It's hard enough to be happy and make a marriage work. Obviously, not all men will be debt-free or without any money problems, but it's important that he at least be responsible in paying his bills.

Is he too frugal?   It can be very frustrating being with a man who is so frugal that it's ridiculous. I once saw a man on a talk show who was a millionaire, and yet he would wait in the parking lot of a particular bakery for 4:00 P.M. to roll around, which was when the doughnuts went on sale! You may be able to accept someone like that—this man's wife didn't seem to have too much of a problem with it. But I think it's better to find someone with balance.

A man who is too frugal can make a woman feel as though he doesn't care about her needs. He's more concerned with saving a buck. He denies her of certain needs and desires that are very important to her, which doesn't make her feel cherished.

Does he spend foolishly?   I once dated a man who didn't have a lot of money yet spent as though there was an unlimited supply. He didn't seem to be the least bit concerned that he was creating a large debt for himself. I began to wonder, "What if I married this man? Would he foolishly spend all our money and not plan for the future?" It's a scary thought. Sometimes this type of behavior can be very selfish, because other's lives are affected. If he has children, then he obviously isn't considering their needs. The money he is throwing away now could be used for their education or other needs down the road.

Is he organized and does he plan ahead?   A man who is good with money has a system for managing his money and knows how to plan ahead. He doesn't have a stack of bills that just lay there for weeks or months. He looks to the future and anticipates how much he will need and when. He is thoughtful about these responsibilities, and he takes them seriously.

A Good Father

As you are looking for a lifetime mate, you will want to carefully consider what kind of father he would be. Sometimes you can get a feeling about this, but there are specific traits you can observe in him.

How does he interact with children?   Try to determine if he even *likes* children. Some men are natural family men and look forward to having children, whereas other men can take them or leave them. Madeline married at thirty-nine and desperately wanted a child. Her husband had no desire for children, but agreed to have a child because of Madeline's strong desire. Madeline ended up doing everything for the child; her husband had little interest. This put more of a burden on her, and made child-rearing a lonely experience. You might want to seek out a man who wants to participate and who, like yourself, is looking forward to being a parent.

Is he fair and just?   A good father will listen to all sides and will strive to come up with solutions (with his wife) that will benefit everyone. He doesn't just rule with an iron fist. He is open-minded and can admit when he is wrong. Look for these traits as you are dating the man in your life. If he is like this generally, then most likely he will be this way with your children.

Will he be available?   A good father is available to his children. They need a father who is there not just physically, but in spirit. It's sad to hear grown men and women say that their fathers were never around because they were too busy with their careers. They may have made a lot of money and gained a lot of prestige, but their children suffered greatly. I should mention that there are times when a family must make sacrifices—for example when times are hard and the father needs to work two or three jobs, naturally diminishing his time with the children. This is when mom has to be even more supportive and fill in as best she can.

Is he firm?   Children need this quality in a father. They won't feel secure without it, and they'll most likely turn into little terrors. They need to know that there are boundaries, and a strong father can help with this. Children need to respect their fathers. This gives them a feeling of stability and order in their lives.

Is he loving and affectionate?   This is probably the most essential quality any parent can have. My uncle Garth, who has ten children, says, "You've got to *drown* your children in love. They have got to know that you adore them." Children, especially babies, need large doses of affection. When children get a little older, they don't always want their parents kissing them, but raising children with regular hugs is essential. Watch and see how demonstrative he is naturally. Is he lovable and cuddly, or is he rather cold?

Is he a good teacher?   Is he the type of man who would be interested in teaching his children important principles in life or how to function effectively in the world? Would he be willing to help them with their homework, or would he be too busy? Most men love to impart their knowledge and expertise to others, especially their children. But some men just aren't into it. Children need guidance, and unless you want to be the sole one to give it to them, you will want to find a man who is looking forward to being a teacher to them.

Can he provide guidance?   Children need to feel secure in knowing they can turn to their parents for direction. They need a father who has the answers or is willing to find the answers rather than saying something like, "I don't know, go ask your mother." (There will be times when he'll say that and it's okay.)

Is he dependable?   A good father can be trusted. His word is his bond. When he says he is going to do something, he does it. This is a quality that is essential to being a good father, not to mention a good mate, a good employee, and a good person.

Is he sensitive?   A good father cares about his children's thoughts and feelings. He will patiently listen to them, no matter how long it takes them to express themselves. He really *cares* about what they have to say and doesn't push them away. He tries to fulfill their needs and even little requests that seem insignificant to him, but which are crucial to the child. Notice how he listens to you to get an idea of what he is like in this area.

Knows How to Treat a Woman

Ask any man if he understands women and you will undoubtedly get a puzzled look and a comment like,

"What, are you *kidding?!*" There are, however, some men who instinctively seem to know how to treat a woman. Maybe their mothers or past girlfriends taught them. But who cares, as long as they know? If you can find a man who understands the nature of a woman, you will be making your life a thousand times easier.

Consider these qualities in judging how he'll treat you over time.

He allows you to express your feelings and emotions. It is wonderful when a man shows patience and understanding when we are trying to express ourselves. Sometimes men wish women could be more like men. But the fact is, most women communicate and express their feelings very differently than men do. It's comforting to be with a man who not only understands that we sometimes have overwhelming feelings and emotions, yet who feels we have a right to express them.

Sometimes we cry or worry, or our feelings get hurt for some reason. I dated a man who asked me quite regularly how I was feeling and then would sit quietly and listen to me as I told him. It was wonderful. If your man consistently tries to listen and be understanding, then chances are you have found a gem.

He makes you his partner. No matter how traditional your relationship may be, most of us want to be considered a partner in life with our mate. He may be a very strong man with strong leadership skills and a desire to be the head of the house, but it's the *spirit* and *attitude* of the man that counts. Does he view you as his slave who is there simply to fulfill his needs, or does he view you as his lifetime partner who will be by his side and participate in decisions that will affect both of you and your children?

He gives you space.   When you get married, you lose some of your freedom. You can't just come and go as you please or take off on a trip somewhere. You've got to consider your mate. Most men are quite protective of their wives and want them nearby. They want them to be available. Sometimes, if overdone, this can get pretty stifling. You want to find a man who is secure enough to give you a certain amount of space and freedom if this is important to you.

He cares about what's important to you.   Every year for Christmas, my father brought home a miserable, little, scrawny tree for the house. And every year, I cried and asked why we couldn't have a big, pretty tree like everyone else. My father didn't mean to hurt me, he just didn't see why it was such a big deal. But small, heartfelt desires can mean the world to us. If you can find a man who understands what's important to you, the easier it will be to feel cherished.

He pampers and spoils you.   We all enjoy getting flowers, little gifts, cards with romantic words written on them, and other mementos of love and affection. Whether he spoils you with words, gifts, or attentiveness, it can greatly add to your happiness. This kind of treatment makes a woman feel special and loved. I'm not talking about excessiveness here. Being spoiled is one thing, but being a spoiled *brat* is another. Most men love to make women happy and enjoy giving them their heart's desire. The more they love you, the more they will be driven to pamper you—they will feel compelled to do it.

Be careful, however, not to *ask* for this kind of treatment. If he doesn't give it to you on his own, then either you will need to look at how you are treating him, or you will need to determine if you can accept a man who doesn't have this nature. Men will give what they want to give or what they are inspired to give. To ask for it directly diminishes the spirit of his giving.

I also suggest that you don't accept expensive gifts until the relationship is very solid, and the two of you have expressed feelings of love. A man could easily get the wrong message, otherwise. If you accept his gifts, he may think you are much more serious than you might be. Also some men *expect* affection, including sex, if they spend a lot of money on a woman. If you've been given an expensive gift early in the relationship, try saying something like, "Thank you so much, but I just can't accept such an expensive gift at this point in our relationship. Can we put gift giving on hold for awhile?" As difficult as this is to say, it sure beats feeling indebted to a man when neither you— nor the relationship—are ready. One woman I know accepted a loan from the new man in her life, and, as a result, the sexual pressure was more than she could bear. He felt more and more that she was "his" and that she owed him.

As you are dating, you want to feel free—free to say no when he asks you out or to date other men if you aren't committed. When money and gifts get involved too soon, the whole relationship becomes overly complicated.

He is understanding. No woman wants to hear something like, "Get with it! You've got it better than most!" We want a man who can understand what we are going through and who we are. When we are down, we want him to put his arms around us and say, "Everything is going to be all right. I know you're frustrated. I'm here for you." A man who is overly critical of mistakes and flaws can make any woman crazy. It's a form of abuse, and no woman should have to tolerate that. You want a man who is accepting of you and who is not constantly pointing out your deficiencies. Ideally, it would be great to find a man who even thinks your little flaws are cute and adorable.

He is loving and affectionate. Most women I know love lots of affection. You will need to find a man who is compatible with you in this area. Every woman has a very deep need to know that she is loved. A man who never verbally expresses his love makes for a very cold partner. You end up feeling empty. No matter how in love you may be with the man, you will feel alone at times. It's been said that men fall in love through their eyes, and women fall in love through their ears. We need to *hear* loving, tender words. We need to hear "I love you" on a regular basis. One man I dated came over to me as I was napping on the couch and gave me a tender kiss on the cheek and stroked my hair in the most gentle way. He thought I was asleep, but I'll never forget how wonderful that small gesture made me feel.

Other Considerations

The traits or qualities covered up to this point I have deemed essential. What follows are other areas to consider.

Lifestyle. His lifestyle reflects how you will be living your life day to day, the kinds of people you will associate with, and where you will go. It's easy to determine compatibility in this area as you date him. The kinds of places he takes you, where he lives, how he spends his vacations, and who he spends his time with are all indicators of what your life together would be like.

Religion. If religion is important to you, then this is a crucial area to consider. Religious beliefs run deep for many people and being committed to someone who disagrees with your beliefs can be very frustrating and painful. Ask yourself the following:

Does he belong to a particular religion?

How important is it to him?

If not part of a particular religion, does he believe in God?

Does God play a role in his life?

Does he believe in prayer, and does he pray? How often?

How would beliefs affect his approach to child rearing?

Is he concerned with the afterlife or only the here and now?

Is it important to him that you share the same religion?

Extended Family. Spend some time getting to know his family. This may not be the most important area to consider, but his family may affect your relationship. As you get to know him, determine the answers to these questions:

Does he get along with his family?

What is their level of influence? (Is he able to make decisions without their consent or influence? Are they a huge part of his life?)

Is there potential of one or more of his family members moving in with him now or in the future?

Does he have ex-wives and/or children from a previous marriage? (And, if so, what are the answers to the questions above?)

After having met his family members, ex-wives, and children, how well do you get along with them? Do you feel they are kind people who would welcome you into their lives?

If you have children from a previous marriage, how does he treat them?

Politics.   Many couples do not agree politically yet still have very good relationships. You should be aware, however, of his political beliefs in your search for compatibility.

Goals/Dreams.   What are his dreams, if any? Do they coincide with your dreams? What does he want to accomplish in life, and does he have a plan for it?

Lisa was very impressed with Bob because of his level of ambition. He wanted to change the world and help a lot of people. His goal was to raise a lot of money in order to accomplish his goals. Lisa had complete faith in him. Over the next couple years, however, Lisa discovered that Bob was a dreamer. He didn't even come *close* to realizing his dreams, because he never took any action toward those goals. It wasn't that he didn't do what he said he wanted to do that bothered Lisa so much. It was that he was so out of touch with reality. She didn't stop loving him, but she did learn that just because someone *says* he is going to be successful or accomplish something, that doesn't mean it will happen. You will want to look at his *actions,* and not just listen to his words.

Also, consider whether or not his goals conflict with yours. If you are out to save the forests and he cuts down trees for a living, then you have got a problem. Make sure you can support him as he strives to make his dreams come true, and that he will be supportive of your goals and dreams as well.

Finding Mr. Right

I realize it isn't easy to meet men, especially men you would consider marrying. If I knew the answer to this question, I wouldn't be single. So although I can't tell you *where* to meet him, I can share tools with you so that once you do meet him, you will know what to do. I used to follow this standard advice: "Get out there and be social, go to parties, join a club or organization, join a dating service! He's not going to show up on your doorstep, you know!" Well, the only thing that happened for me was that I ended up spending a lot of money on events that bored me to death. I wanted to leave the minute I got there, and I never met anyone I wanted to date. Although I do believe you need to be out there in order to meet people, I don't think it's absolutely necessary to go out there and *make* it happen. (As an aside, I believe church—or your friends from church—offers the best avenue to meet good men.)

If You Are Ready, He'll Appear

In the movie *Field of Dreams,* the main character, played by Kevin Costner, kept hearing voices whispering, "If you build it, they will come." So he built an incredible baseball diamond in the middle of his field, and when it was finished, sure enough, the spirits of several famous baseball players appeared.

Now as corny as this may sound, I believe that when we are ready, our mates will appear. I attend a church service every Sunday that is made up of all single people. Most of us there experience the same fears: We think we will never meet the right person, we will grow old without ever getting married and live a very lonely existence. But over the past couple years, there have been many, many marriages. Some of those same people who felt totally hopeless, one day met their mate and now they are married. And I believe the rest of us will be married at some point also. *What we need to focus on is preparing ourselves for marriage.* We need to do all the things we want to do while we're single, because we may not have a chance once we are married. I know very few people who never marry. It's just a matter of time for us.

14

Awakening Love *Before* Getting Physical

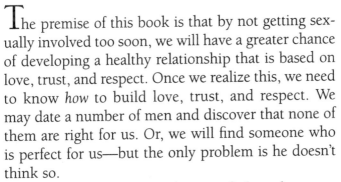

The premise of this book is that by not getting sexually involved too soon, we will have a greater chance of developing a healthy relationship that is based on love, trust, and respect. Once we realize this, we need to know *how* to build love, trust, and respect. We may date a number of men and discover that none of them are right for us. Or, we will find someone who is perfect for us—but the only problem is he doesn't think so.

Let's say the day comes when you feel you have met someone very special, and you think he may be the one. He seems to like you just as much as you like him, although you aren't sure. All you know is, you don't want to mess this one up. You have already made your Personal Pledge so you know sex won't get in the way of finding out if this will be true love. There are, however, so many other considerations. We want to be ourselves, but we don't want to scare him away. The question is, Is there anything we can do to awaken feelings of love in this man, or do we simply rely on luck, nature, or destiny?

The Art of Awakening Love

You do have the power to awaken love. You do not have to hope or wish for it to "click." The power is within us. It's only a matter of tapping into it. This doesn't mean that men aren't partly responsible, but to put the failure or success of our relationship in someone else's hands is not going to give us what we want. If we make him responsible, our relationship is susceptible to too many factors outside our control. We don't have the power to change anyone or control their behavior, but there is a lot we can do in the way of creating a harmonious relationship.

There is an art to awakening feelings of love within the man we choose. As we apply this art to our relationship, we will be amazed at how differently he responds to us and how much stronger our relationship becomes. Our life becomes a life of joy rather than the heartache of continued break-ups.

Many women throughout the world are cherished and loved by their husbands and boyfriends. Some of them may have never read a book in their lives about how to create the love they have. Either they instinctively knew how to create a harmonious, loving relationship, or possibly their mothers, sisters, or friends explained various methods that work.

Then there are women who are either married or are in relationships in which they aren't cherished and loved as they should be. Their mates may care very much for them and even be completely committed to them. But they don't *cherish* them.

All of these women may be equally attractive or intelligent. They all have their strengths and weaknesses. So what's the difference?

The difference is that some women *live* the principles. They naturally possess the qualities described in chapter 12, and they seem intuitively to understand men. They have a way about them that draws out the best in a man. Men find them adorable, delightful, and fascinating. Sometimes these women are aware of which behaviors and traits draw men to them and sometimes they are oblivious to them.

The smartest thing a woman can do for herself is study the underlying principles that create and awaken true love so that she can approach a relationship with confidence and purpose rather than simply hoping things will work out.

Is This Being Manipulative?

Men and women are different. Each of us have inherent qualities which awaken specific feelings in the opposite sex. There is nothing wrong with getting in touch with these natural qualities and using them to enhance our relationship with the opposite sex. That's why they are there. When men compliment us on how nice we look, we don't feel they are being manipulative (even if they are). We just love the fact that they *said* it.

We want men to understand us and our natures, don't we? We want that special person to buy us flowers and tell us how nice we look, even if it doesn't come easily to him. It makes us feel good. Many, if not most, men understand this.

The only time any of the suggestions in this book could be considered manipulative is if they are applied insincerely or with evil intent. If we are trying to capture a man just for our own ego needs or some other selfish motive, then we will need to reevaluate our priorities. This book is designed to provide basic information on how to awaken true love with the man of our choice, but it's only meant to be used with the highest standards and best intentions.

How to Tell If He Is in Love with You

When a man is in love, he can't seem to get the woman out of his mind. As hard as he tries, he cannot seem to live without her. He finds himself doing more for her and with her than anyone else. He is compelled to be with her, to give to her, to call her, to think of her, and to protect her. He is also sexually drawn to her and wants to be affectionate with her. But when a man truly loves a woman, he will respect her feelings when it comes to sex. He would never want to hurt her. In fact, he has an overwhelming desire to make her happy.

Although he may fight expressing his feelings in the beginning, he eventually *must* express his love. He finds he can't hold back. Being in love brings him great joy and inspires him to be a better man. It gives him a reason to be more successful and more responsible.

The more in love a man is, the more he will give. He will give more of his time, attention, and money. The look in his eyes will also give it away. In the movie *Shadowlands*, the character played by Debra Winger said to Anthony Hopkins, "Now you look at me properly," when it became obvious that he was deeply in love with her. You could just see the love welling up in his eyes.

He will begin to take the relationship more seriously. He won't want to keep the relationship a secret, he will want to shout it from the rooftops. Once we experience this kind of love, we will never want to settle for anything less.

What Men Fall in Love With

Men usually do not know why or how they fall in love, they only know that they feel wonderful when they are with us. It's a mystery for most men and women, but it doesn't have to be. Some people are just not meant to be together and no matter what, love is not going to grow. In most cases, however, there is much within our control. To simplify the process, it could be said that men fall in love with two things: *Who we are* and *what we do.*

Who We Are.   We covered the qualities we want to develop within ourselves in chapter 12. If we strive to develop our feminine nature and become adorable, fresh, radiant women, men will be drawn to us.

If we think in terms of *inner* and *outer* qualities, we can easily remember what we are striving for. The inner qualities include calmness, peacefulness, happiness, understanding, high self-esteem, and having a strong character.

The outer qualities refer to our appearance, which should be feminine, soft, neat, clean, and modest. We need to maintain a healthy, radiant glow, sparkling eyes, and clear skin. Plus, always wear a big smile. Other outer qualities are being spunky, outspoken, playful, and charming.

All these qualities will attract men to us, enhance our relationships, and bring us more joy. But being a wonderful woman is often not enough. There are plenty of incredible women who don't have men knocking down their doors to get at them. Who we are is important, but equally important is *what we do*.

What We Do. Most relationships don't last, and even the ones that do, aren't always happy. Love will not always just happen naturally. We may do things that completely prevent love from fully developing.

You may be beautiful, charming, intelligent, and witty. But if you don't know how to treat a man, you probably won't be able to hold on to him for long. You certainly won't have the kind of love described in chapter 1.

As we treat a man with respect, appreciate all that he does for us, admire his strengths, and learn to trust him, he naturally falls in love with us. The more consistently we fulfill his needs (and ensure that our own needs are met), the deeper the love grows. We can create a beautiful relationship with a man by following the Five Basic Rules for Dating listed in chapter 8 and maintaining that sense of mystery and challenge.

Why He Might Not Be Falling in Love

Relationships can be very complex. There isn't always a simple answer. The following reasons show why he might *not* be falling in love.

1. *You don't have chemistry.* Sometimes a relationship is just not meant to be. Everything may be clicking for you, but he is not feeling the same way. If this happens, just move on. There is very little, if anything, we can do in this situation. Sometimes two people can become attracted to

each other over time, but my experience has been that if the chemistry isn't there in the beginning, it probably won't be there later.

2. *We're chasing him too much.* Remember, men are the natural pursuers. It ruins the flow of the process when we turn the tables and begin doing their job. Men lose their motivation.

   The relationship is not necessarily ruined if we have made the mistake of chasing him. We simply need to stop pursuing him. We should stop calling him (except to return his calls). We shouldn't ask him out, initiate affection, hint about or bring up the relationship, or ask where it is going. It also wouldn't hurt for us to be a little too busy to see him at times. The idea is to *create interest* once again. Most of the time we can start over, and, if maintained, we can get back on track.

   Note: If a man says something like, "Why don't you give me a call tomorrow?", unless he's your boyfriend, I suggest you respond with, "I'd prefer it if you called me." Don't be afraid to gently put the responsibility back on him, even though he may seem put off at first. Men like women who insist that they do the pursuing.

3. *We lack certain qualities that men find desirable in women.* I know a woman who gets plenty of sexual attention from men, but no one wants a serious relationship with her. She is loud, at times very obnoxious, pushy, and very opinionated. She also dresses provocatively and has an extremely sexy look. Yet, she can't understand why men don't want her for anything but sex. The saddest part is that this woman isn't willing

to look at herself and admit that changes need
to be made.

We need to study chapter 12 and identify
those areas we need to work on. We must remember that most men want a woman who is
feminine, smart, healthy, happy, peaceful, honest, loving, and strong. We can also ask close
friends what they think about our personality,
looks, or character that might need some re-
vamping. The truth can sometimes hurt, but so
does rejection.

4. *We don't make him feel great when he's with us.* In
   the next section, we are going to cover the nine
   basic needs of a man. If these needs aren't met
   fairly consistently, he may not be able to fall
   deeply in love. He may like you a lot or grow to
   care for you, but he won't feel love in the deepest
   sense. A man needs to feel respected, appreciated, admired, and understood. If he doesn't, he
   may not be inspired to make you his lifetime
   partner. If you find yourself criticizing him, however subtly, or you like to argue, control, or attempt to change him, you need to study the next
   section very carefully and try making changes in
   the way you treat all men; especially the man you
   are seeing romantically.

5. *He is incapable of loving anyone.* Some men, no
   matter who you are or what you do, are simply
   unable to open up and actually love someone.
   Perhaps they suffered from severe childhood
   trauma. Although people can change and overcome these difficulties, the last thing you want
   to do is spend a lifetime trying to get someone

to love you who just isn't capable. Moving on is the best choice.

6. *It has nothing to do with us.* Bad timing could be why some men won't allow themselves to fall in love. They just refuse to open up to the possibilities because of something else going on in their lives. Perhaps he is seeing another woman or still trying to get over a past relationship. There could be any number of reasons. If you suspect this could be the case, you may want to ask him what's troubling him (you only need to ask once, then drop it if he doesn't want to discuss the issue). If you ask him with a caring, understanding attitude, he probably will open up. If your hunch was right, then all you can do is be patient (if you are willing to wait). You could simply be a friend until things change. It's definitely a good idea to date other men in the meantime.

How to Make Him Feel Like a Million Bucks

Men fall in love with us as we supply them with what their souls cry out for. As we admire him for his strengths, appreciate all he does, show him understanding, and give him respect, a man becomes completely devoted to us. It is difficult to give a man these things consistently, but the more consistently we fulfill his needs, the more consistently we will feel cherished. Men do not expect this kind of treatment all the time; however, a woman who is aware that this is what men need and who strives to give this to her man will be seen as an angel.

The mistake many women make is by being overly concerned with what they are *getting* out of the relationship rather than having confidence that their needs will be met beyond all expectations when they give men what they need.

HIS NINE BASIC NEEDS

Respect

A man must feel respected, especially by the woman he loves. Women want to be respected also, but in a different way and to a different degree. For a man to thrive and be happy, he must have the respect of the woman in his life. When a woman doesn't really respect a man, she often begins to destroy him. This may be quite obvious or very subtle. It usually begins with little criticisms. She may get irritated with the way he does things or his views on a situation. She doesn't fully trust him. She doesn't really respect his judgment or leadership abilities.

Many extremely successful men credit their success to the women in their lives. Truly amazing things can happen when a man is inspired by a wise, good woman.

How to Show Respect

I was having dinner with some friends of mine. I'll call them Cheri and William. They have been married for about a year. I have never seen them argue. As I observed them, I could see why. They were trying to decide on a particular investment. William thought it was an excellent opportunity, while Cheri felt it was too risky. The way Cheri chose to handle the situation was perfect. She didn't criticize him or his idealistic views. She didn't roll her eyes or make fun of him. She didn't argue his points. She simply said, "I feel a little nervous about the risk involved, but I trust your judgment. You seem to know more about these particular investments than I do, and I'm sure you will do the right thing." This attitude made him feel respected and loved, and he was spared from being embarrassed in front of an outside person. Cheri called me a few weeks later to tell me that William chose not to invest because, as she said, "He didn't want to do something that would make me feel uneasy."

As this example illustrates, the main principle behind showing him respect is *trusting his judgment*. If we are with a man whose judgment we cannot trust, we need to reconsider our choice of men.

We need to make it a rule to never argue on and on with a man. It's okay to disagree and even to debate if it's in the right spirit, but it's better to *agree to disagree*, while still letting him know that we respect him.

Admiration

Just as we need to be cherished, men need to be admired. This is obvious and yet so few women ever really practice this. First of all, we are afraid he'll expect this kind of treatment all the time, and we're not sure we are up to it. Then there's the problem of feeling phony or silly. But as we practice looking for things to admire in men, we see the pleasure it gives them. Admiration brings so much joy to the relationship. The added work is such a small investment considering the great return.

Men crave admiration. They long for it. They need it. And the woman who gives it to them is the one they will adore forever. It is rare for a man, especially these days, to find a woman who will show him admiration. And when he does find a woman who sees his strengths and actually comments on them, it's as though he's found a hidden treasure. He will long to be with her more and more. She becomes central to his happiness.

Many women today are too busy trying to get respect and admiration for themselves. They have their own accomplishments for which to seek attention. They figure, "Why should *I* work so hard to make him look good? What about *me*?" Women who feel this way obviously have never experienced the rewards of giving men the admiration they need. They see it as more work than it's worth, rather than a simple, easy thing to do for the return of tender love and a positive relationship. The most awesome advantage of showing admiration is that the more it is given, the more our love and appreciation for each other grows.

The more sincere admiration we give a man, the more he will want to be with us simply because of the way he feels when he is with us. One rule that must always be followed is that the admiration must be sincere; dissembling will backfire.

How to Show Admiration

We can always find masculine qualities to admire in any man. Look for things that really have meaning to him. Men are not all that moved if we only admire the way they are dressed or how prompt they are. Look for mental or physical traits, especially those traits that they are particularly proud of.

It is easy to show a man that we admire him, although it may be awkward at first. With a little practice, it will become second nature.

Here are some qualities to admire in him:

His Work. If we encourage him to talk about his work, we will find an entire treasure chest of things to admire. Men take their work very seriously. A man appreciates a woman who is interested in what he does and who finds importance in his work. Men usually carry a lot of burdens and stress in this area of their lives. They strongly need a woman who is willing to listen and sympathize.

Say Things Like: "You really have a lot of responsibility with your job. I'll bet you are very good at what you do." or "How did you get to be so successful? You're so talented."

Find out *why* he does what he does for a living. Men usually have all kinds of dreams, goals, and aspirations that they would love to share with a woman who is interested.

His Athleticism. Maybe he is gifted in athletics. Men love it when women notice their strengths in this area.

Say Things Like: "You are so athletic! I love to watch you in action!"

"You're the best player out there. You're really strong."

His Physique. Admiring a man's body will have a greater effect than anything else. Let him know his masculinity brings out the woman in you.

I realize that some of these comments might seem embarrassing or silly, but as you practice expressing yourself in this way, it will become more natural. And the men will love it. They don't care how corny it is, as long as you mean what you say. They may laugh and tease you at first, but they won't want you to stop!

Say Things Like: "You are so big and strong. I just love your body!"

"I love having your big, strong arms around me. You make me feel so safe."

His Mental Abilities. Men also love it when their intellect is admired. Look for moments when his problem-solving skills come into play, such as his ability to negotiate a deal or the like.

Say Things Like: "I just love the fact that you are so smart. You are a walking encyclopedia!" or "What would I do without you? You are really brilliant!" or "I am so glad you know so much, it makes me feel more secure."

His Overall Masculine Nature. There doesn't have to be a reason or specific occurrence for you to express your appreciation for his masculinity. You can give him a big hug and tell him you love how much of a *man* he is!

I have found that the more we admire the *masculinity* in a man, the more *femininity* he will see in us. This will create a powerful chemistry between you and your mate.

Acceptance

Accepting a man means we accept *everything* about him. Bad habits, little quirks in his personality, the decisions he makes, what he does for a living, how he spends his time, how he deals with his problems, and so on. We may not like every aspect of the man, but we do need to accept him as he is. If we can't accept him as he is, then it is probably in our best interest to move on rather than remain in the relationship and try to change him. There are times, however, when two people can work through their differences. With luck, he is a man who is open to personal growth. We should all be looking for someone who is willing to compromise and who will admit when he is the one who needs to change. However, men need to come to this conclusion on their own, not because of our prodding or insistence that they change. He will only resent us trying to change him.

A man I dated several years ago was open and willing to talk things through. He really listened to my concerns. A few things were bothering me, and I wanted to discuss them with him. He listened intently, nodding, holding my hand. When I finished, he said he heard me, and that he was really going to make an effort to change. And he did make an effort, for awhile. But the bottom line is, *he ended up being who he really was and who he really wanted to be.* Only now I had created a wall between us. He knew that I didn't see him as my knight in shining armor anymore and that I wanted him to be different. This affected his feelings for me. Eventually we grew further and further apart.

What should I have done? I should have either made a decision to *accept* those qualities fully or ended the relationship. Instead, I chose to stay in the relationship and to try to get him to be someone he wasn't. Even though I did it in a way that would make a therapist proud, it didn't work, and it never has worked for me. *Trying to change a man only succeeds in destroying love.*

What Criticizing
Your Man Will Do

I happen to know first hand the ill-effects of criticizing a man. This habit usually rears its ugly head at some point in the relationship when we think we need to test him or when we realize subconsciously that we are with the wrong person. We feel stuck, usually because we are sexually bonded to the man, which makes walking away very difficult. Instead of leaving, we start criticizing. We have a bad attitude because we are unhappy, thus, criticizing him comes naturally. We don't really want to criticize. In fact, as we are criticizing him, we're usually thinking, "I know I shouldn't be doing this. I should just shut up right now before it's too late." We can't seem to help ourselves. We just have this overwhelming, uncontrollable urge to tell him exactly what we think!

Inevitably we end up alienating the very man we want to have cherish and love us! When a man feels that he isn't admired, respected, and appreciated by the woman he loves, he begins to construct a wall. This wall gets thicker in time. Before long, the love that was once there is no longer able to survive. He may love the woman as a person or as the mother of his children, but he won't feel as deeply *in love* as he may have felt in the beginning when she saw him as her hero.

How to Stop Criticizing

When we find the right person and surrender to the relationship, it is easier not to be critical. We can, however, still find ourselves falling into the habit.

Overcoming being critical takes practice. After we lose a few good men because of our critical natures, not criticizing becomes a little easier. But a critical attitude has its roots in one's character. To develop a loving, nonjudgmental character, one has to grow spiritually and learn to be happy within. As we learn to love and accept ourselves, we are more easily able to love and accept others.

Appreciation

If we want a man to cherish us, we will want to show him a lot of appreciation. What do I mean by appreciation? Letting him know through our words and actions that we appreciate who he is and all that he does for us. Appreciation and admiration go hand in hand. Giving him the clear impression that we like him just the way he is and that he is our hero makes him feel very appreciated, which in turn will make you feel very loved.

Men often say, "She just seemed to *expect* it." A man wants to give himself to a woman, but he has a serious problem if she just expects this treatment and isn't really appreciative. Think about the times you have given someone a gift or have done something special for them. If they thanked you, praised you, or loved it, then you received more pleasure, right?

I know a man who was constantly buying his girlfriend gifts for no particular reason. I asked him what it was that compelled him to do this. He said, "Whenever I give my girlfriend anything, whether it's expensive or not, she just loves it and appreciates it so much. I just can't wait to do it again and again. It makes me feel great!"

How to Show Appreciation

In showing a man appreciation, look for opportunities to say how glad we are that he is a part of our life. Don't allow moments to slip by where we can show gratitude and give praise when he does something nice for us. Then we can *show* him how much we appreciate him by doing nice things for *him*. There are many ways we can give back. Men love it when we cook for them. Small gifts are okay at times, but most men prefer we do something nice for them rather than spend money.

Say Things Like: "You are so good to me. How did I get to be so lucky?" or "You really are my knight in shining armor! Thank you for being so generous." Even if you do not like the particular present he gave you, he will appreciate your thanking him for the gesture.

Cooperation

A man appreciates a woman who is flexible and cooperates with him. Unfortunately, being cooperative isn't so easy to do, especially when we think our way is better. That's another reason why it is so important to find someone with whom we are highly compatible—it's easier to avoid power struggles. The sad part is that most of the situations in which we become stubborn or difficult are usually unimportant in the scheme of things.

Men need cooperation for many reasons. I'm not suggesting that we subordinate ourselves to men simply for the sake of keeping the peace. All women should speak their mind, maintain their own opinions, and be their own person. But if we want *harmony* in our relationship and our goal is obtaining the highest level of love, then we will have to find ways to show some level of cooperation in dealing with men. Men don't want a woman who fights them at every turn.

I have found that most of the times when I just didn't want to cooperate with a man was because I was with the wrong man. We just weren't compatible. Either I didn't respect his views or I didn't like the way he approached life in general. The bottom line was, I wasn't happy being with him and that unhappiness came out in the form of not being cooperative.

I have found it to be more effective to show disappointment and hurt rather than to yell, berate, or argue. It's okay to be angry and to express that anger. But screaming, being irate, and showing hostility are never very effective. How often have we been totally justified in being angry with a man only to alienate him?

When we express hurt or disappointment, a man will gather us up in his arms and tells us he is sorry for hurting us. There is a proverb that says: "By fighting you never get enough, but by yielding you get more than you expected."

How to Be Cooperative

We need to ask ourselves if what we are fighting for is really worth it. If we did it his way, then would we be violating our own moral standards? If we are not violating our standards, then why not try to be flexible and see what happens? We may want to save our energy for when we do feel strongly about having our own way. Even if we disagree, we can choose to support him in his decision.

We do this not to acquiesce, but to show our love, understanding, and trust in our man. Our relationship isn't a competition where you each fight for equal rights. We want to do our part no matter what the other person is doing, simply because we love them and want to create a beautiful relationship that is healthy and harmonious.

Say Something Like: "I would prefer to do it this way, but if you feel that strongly about it, I will support you in your decision."

Trust

A man was walking along and fell off a cliff. As he was falling, he grabbed onto a vine that was sticking out of the mountain. There he was, suspended, holding onto the vine for dear life. He cried out to God, "God, please save me!" He heard a voice, "Let go of the vine, and ye shall be free." He looked around and saw no one. Again he cried, "God, please save me!" Again he heard the voice, "Let go of the vine, and ye shall be free." He looked down and cried out again, "God, please help me!" The voice repeated the same words, "Let go of the vine, and ye shall be free." The man looked up at the sky and said, "Is anyone *else* up there?!"

It's difficult to surrender to anything or anyone. I'd like to share a story with you about a woman I know who has never trusted men and certainly has never surrendered to one. But once she did, she saw the difference. "I was so tired of nit-picking about meaningless things with Andrew. I had been saying I was going to leave him for two years, yet I stayed. So I decided to stop saying I was leaving, and just surrender to the relationship. The minute I did that, Andrew began talking marriage. There was such a huge difference in the way he treated me. He told me he loved me more often. He would call me during the day just to see how I was doing. He was much more loving. I guess he couldn't fully love me before because he sensed my lack of commitment. He saw that I always had one foot out the door. Once he saw that I had really surrendered to the relationship, the floodgates opened, and it has been wonderful."

We don't want to totally surrender who we are, and we don't want to surrender too soon. But we do want to let go and trust our man slowly throughout the relationship, and at deeper levels, the longer we are together. When we show a man that we trust him, it causes him to want to rise to the occasion and not let us down.

How to Show Trust

The best way to show a man that we trust him is to just sit back and allow him to lead. It's already within his nature to do so; therefore, it requires very little on our part. Let him take care of things for a change. We can initially do this as an experiment, simply to see what happens and how he responds to our new attitude. We don't need to tell him what we are doing. We should just do it. We can give him the freedom to make most of the decisions and do things his way as much as possible. If we don't like the choices he makes and the way he does things, then there is a chance we are with the wrong person. Or, we may need to say something like, "I'm just not comfortable doing that. Could you come up with another idea?"

Sometimes we make the mistake of thinking that we have to control everything and take over. We are afraid certain things won't get done. This is rarely the case. It's just that we have never backed off long enough to show him that we trust him. Once we do, he will then have the space to take action. When we don't back off we make him feel inadequate and not needed. Men become more passive until we assume that they are lazy. We soon think that they always leave everything to us, which just isn't the case.

I know a woman who has had a few bad experiences with men. She now appears to be paranoid. She's afraid he won't call when he says he will. She feels she has to get him to verbally commit to when they will see each other again. This, of course, kills feelings of trust and puts a real strain on him and on the relationship.

Freedom

We all want to feel as though we are able to be who we want to be, do what we want to do, and believe what we want to believe. Men can't stand to feel confined, tied down, or pressured. It's more the *feeling* of freedom they love than anything else.

We should never act like we own the man we are with. Men will devote themselves to us, but they don't want us to make them feel they are imprisoned.

We should never tell a man what to do. I see a lot of women bossing their men around and making suggestions as to how something should be done. Men not only don't appreciate this, they get turned off by it. They deliberately may do the opposite of what we suggest just to prove that they can't be controlled.

Don't Try To Control Him

We try to control men by telling them —subtly or overtly—what to do. We make suggestions, hints, or outright demands. We sometimes try to manipulate them into doing it our way. We basically try to run their lives.

Very few men like being controlled. Many, if not most, men will not put up with it from the outset. Others may seemingly accept it for awhile, but all men eventually will begin to resent the woman who tries to control them. Instead of love growing and deepening, it begins to be destroyed little by little.

For the sake of your relationship, don't try to control him. Instead, try accepting him as he is and allow him the freedom to be his own man. He will adore you when you do.

How to Give Him Freedom

Here is a checklist of ways to give a man freedom.

- Don't quiz him, nag him, try to get him to call, or see you according to your timetable and desires. Let him decide for himself when he wants to be with you.

- Don't tell him how he should be spending his time and don't make plans for him without consulting with him first.

- Don't hint about a future together unless you are engaged. This can make him feel trapped by someone who wants to take him over.

- Don't worry about him when he is not with you. Keep in mind that he is a big boy and can take care of himself. Men don't want to marry their mothers—healthy ones, that is!

Understanding

Travis, a real estate developer, had just purchased his first big deal—a piece of property in a prime location where he could build a shopping center. He had worked hard for years for this opportunity. He had to put as much energy as possible into the project. Jaleen, his girlfriend, didn't seem to understand the importance of Travis's work. She constantly tried to distract him. She would call his office incessantly, insisting that he spend more time with her. If he were late due to extended meetings, then he knew he'd be in big trouble.

Travis really cared about Jaleen and wanted to be with her, but sometimes he just couldn't break away from his project. He had a lot of responsibility, and he wished she was more supportive. He tried to explain his position, but Jaleen couldn't shake the feeling of being neglected. She couldn't see the situation from his perspective, she only saw her own. They fought a lot about the issue until Travis finally began pulling away. The relationship with Jaleen brought more aggravation than he could tolerate in his life.

When I used to sell commercial real estate, I gained a very good sense of what many men go through. The pressures and responsibilities can be enormous, not to mention the unexpected problems that arise. A man desperately needs a mate who is very understanding and supportive in this area.

When he calls and says he will be late or even cancels a date with you, imagine the difference in how he will feel about you when you say something like, "It's okay, I understand. You take care of the problems at work, I'll talk to you tomorrow." versus "I can't believe you're doing this to me *again!* How can you cancel on me at the last minute?! What am I supposed to do now?"

As he works into the night and then drives home, which response will have him tenderly thinking about you, wanting to see you? An understanding attitude causes a man to want to see you as soon as possible, simply to be with the woman he loves.

Encouragement

By encouraging a man, we give him the clear message that we believe in him and that we are behind him, no matter what. We are the positive force in his life when he feels down. The more we give a man encouragement, the more he will turn to us. We want our mate to come to us with his goals, his triumphs, his defeats. This is what builds a bond between two people and adds depth to a relationship.

Encouragement is important in making a man feel as though you are truly on his side and behind him every step of the way. He needs to know that you believe in him and that you have faith in his abilities. He will begin to feel that you are the one woman who really knows how to build him up and encourage him.

How to Show Encouragement

When a man expresses fears, doubts, worries, or disappointments, we can then encourage him by saying something like, "I know you are going to do great. You are so smart and capable. I know you will do the right thing. I believe in you."

We don't want to give him advice or try to solve his problems. We do want to focus on encouraging him as a way to help instill confidence. He will figure out his own solutions. Right now he just needs an encouraging friend who believes in him.

Don't Give Too Much!

Even though I believe you should give men what they need, you don't want to give too much. If you focus only on pleasing him, serving him, and making him happy, he will get spoiled. This is not healthy for a relationship. He will begin to take advantage of you. His feelings for you will begin to cool, and, of course, you'll feel used. Your inner voice and intuition will let you know when to pull back and give less.

How to Deal with Him When He Seems Distant or Cold

If a man seems aloof, we may have given too much. We may have tried to control him, or not shown our appreciation for what he has done for us. Perhaps it has nothing to do with us. In any case, we need to back off and give him some space, while at the same time letting him know that we do appreciate him. During this time, we can focus on our own interests and life. He will eventually come around.

Don't constantly ask him what is wrong. Ask once, of course, in case he is waiting for the opportunity to confide. But after that one time, back off.

How to Get Him to Open Up

A man opens up and expresses his true feelings when he feels safe to do so. The last thing we want to do when he does open up is say something like, "I told you so!" or "Why did you do that?!" Instead, let him know by your words and mannerisms that you care, sympathize, and understand.

Our Part When Falling in Love

When we first meet someone or go out on a first date, either there is chemistry or there isn't. We either connect or we don't. If we don't, that doesn't necessarily mean we never will. Within the first couple dates, both parties decide if they are willing to go further with the relationship.

If you are still willing to go out with him and if he continues to call, then before long, a relationship is formed. There are various phases of a relationship, but through the initial phase—say the first three or four months or until he has expressed that he loves you and is committed to the relationship—each partner plays a certain role. Fulfilling your part is imperative if you want things to work out well. These are general guidelines, especially during this early phase:

His Part

He should do the following:

- The calling
- The asking out
- The expressing of his feelings first

- The bringing up of the relationship and the direction it's going
- The initiating of physical advances

Your Part

You should do the following:

- Be yourself (ideally with the qualities described in chapter 12)
- Slowly reveal the various layers of yourself to him
- Be interested in your own life and not worry about the relationship, where it is going, or what his feelings are
- Be confident that the relationship will evolve and know that he will make it happen
- Look for things in him to admire, appreciate, respect
- Get to know him better to determine if he is someone we can accept exactly as he is
- Share our feelings for him after he shares his feelings for us
- Set the sexual standard

You may think too much emphasis is made on fulfilling *his* needs. "What about my needs?" you may ask. As we follow all the principles outlined in this book, your needs will be met beyond your expectations. When you try to "get," you usually end up with much, much less. When you focus on giving back to a man, as he gives to you, you receive more than you ever would have received had you asked for more. You do have the ability to awaken love in the man you want. As you practice these behaviors and techniques, you will learn what works and what doesn't with different men. And you will see amazing results very quickly.

15

A New Beginning

The journey of life can be extremely difficult at times. After reading about all the rules, standards, pledges, and charts you need to follow, you may be feeling a little overwhelmed. Let me reassure you that just as Rome wasn't built in a day, neither are we expected to transform ourselves instantly. Growth comes in layers. A garden is planted one seed at a time, one row at a time. If the gardener is consistent, eventually the entire garden is planted, and ultimately the gardener reaps the rewards of his labor. As we take the necessary steps to improve ourselves and our lives, we too will reap the rewards of our labor. Should we fall short of our goals or miss a step along the way, we need to pick ourselves up and simply start over rather than criticize or condemn. We should never lose hope.

We want to reach higher and tap into the hidden treasures that await us by following our conscience and remaining on the road that leads us to our desired destination. Although we need to take practical steps along the way, this is a spiritual journey. Rather than seeing sex as we used to, we are now seeing it from a spiritual perspective. We see the wondrous beauty and awesome power that it holds. Where we may have viewed our bodies as simply flesh, we are now beginning to see them as spiritual vessels, whereby we can bring new life into the world and house our own unique spirit. As we take on this spiritual view, we automatically begin taking better care of our mind, body, and spirit.

Once we begin living this new way of life, with this new perspective, a shift takes place. We draw in a higher quality man—one who sees and recognizes the light within us. We have a higher purpose, one that is more divinely inspired. Our relationship will be on a whole new plane, full of tenderness, purpose, and meaning. We begin to live what truly is the "Good Life."

The beautiful part of this process is that once we grow to new levels, we then begin to focus on the world around us. We are no longer bogged down with dysfunctional relationships that sap our energy and squander our precious time. Rather than living a self-centered life, we are able to be a part of making the world around us a better place for us all to live.

We are faced with countless problems in society: Alarmingly high rates of divorce, teenage pregnancies, abortions, AIDS and other sexually transmitted diseases—the list goes on. Overcoming these social ills seems impossible. But we can be part of the solution in our own personal way. By making a shift in our own lives, we absolutely will have a positive impact on the world around us.

There is a movement underway called the Abstinence Movement. Thousands of teenagers all across America are pledging abstinence until they marry. In my research, I found article after article on the dangers and perils of casual sex and how young people need to construct stronger boundaries for themselves. But why is this message only directed to the youth? Whether we are sixteen or sixty, we experience the same heartache with casual sex. And why is the focus primarily on the physical ramifications of having sex? The women I spoke with said that their greatest motivation to abstain is because of emotional reasons.

Abstinence is for all of us. We need to set a whole new standard in America. Ever since the '60s, sex has become expected. Since the majority of women will do "it," where does that leave the rest of us who won't? I believe it puts us in the best position of all. We will be seen as healthy, fascinating, virtuous, and refreshing. Applying the principles in this book is a step in the right direction.

We need always to be true to ourselves. A true modern woman has principles by which she lives. She knows herself, she doesn't pretend to be something she's not. She has accepted herself both past and present, she knows what she wants, and she doesn't compromise her most precious values along the way. She is virtuous and vulnerable. She understands relationships and men. She has searched for knowledge that will aid her in building a strong, solid relationship. She is not perfect, nor does she expect herself to be, but she strives to be the best she can—for herself, her mate, and her future family.

Making love will be a very special part of *the* relationship we will ultimately find ourselves in. I'm talking about the relationship we share with the man we love and respect, and who has proven his love for us. This will be the man with whom we have spent countless hours together, uncovering each other's mysteries, thoughts, and true feelings. This is the man who will be there for us through good times and bad, sickness and health, rain or shine. He will express his undying love for us, as we will do the same for him. Making love will be the icing on the cake.

If we embrace these principles and take our responsibilities seriously, we can and will build a loving relationship that can last forever. The only thing holding us back is our doubts and fears. As women, let's commit together, so that collectively, we can set a whole new standard and give each other the strength and support we need. By doing so, we will surely make the world a better place in which to live.

Index

If you are interested in receiving a free brochure regarding Laurie Langford's seminars, or would like to schedule Laurie for a speaking engagement, please call:

(310) 289-2133

Or write to:

Laurie Langford
505 S. Beverly Drive, Suite 647
Beverly Hills, CA 90212